The Transition to College Writing

The Transition to College Writing

SECOND EDITION

Keith Hjortshoj
Cornell University

Bedford / St. Martin's   Boston ◆ New York

For Bedford/St. Martin's

Developmental Editor: Marisa Feinstein
Production Associate: Samuel Jones
Marketing Manager: Molly Parke
Project Management: Books By Design, Inc.
Text Design: Claire Seng-Niemoeller
Cover Design: Sara Gates
Composition: Books By Design, Inc.
Printing and Binding: RR Donnelley & Sons Company

President: Joan E. Feinberg
Editorial Director: Denise B. Wydra
Editor in Chief: Karen S. Henry
Director of Marketing: Karen R. Soeltz
Director of Editing, Design, and Production: Marcia Cohen
Assistant Director of Editing, Design, and Production: Elise S. Kaiser
Manager, Publishing Services: Emily Berleth

Library of Congress Control Number: 2008934227

Manufactured in the United States of America.

4   3

i   h

For information, write: Bedford/St. Martin's, 75 Arlington Street, Boston, MA 02116   (617-399-4000)

ISBN-10: 0-312-44082-0
ISBN-13: 978-0-312-44082-4

Acknowledgments

Page 123: From Dennis Normile, "Asian Fusions," *Science* 312: 993 (2006). Reprinted with permission from AAAS.

In memory of Jim Slevin

Preface

This second edition of *The Transition to College Writing*, like the first, is based on the premise that the journey from high school to college is not just a step onto a higher rung of the same educational ladder. Instead, going to college offers the opportunity to ascend different ladders altogether: to develop new skills, interests, goals, and relationships in unfamiliar educational environments.

The great majority of students welcome this opportunity. They also know that undergraduate studies will require changes in the ways they approach writing, reading, thinking, and learning. But which strategies need to change? How exactly do they need to change, and why? If we want to preserve the transformative values of higher education, these questions must remain difficult to answer, both for students who are entering college and for their teachers.

In her essay "Whistling in the Dark," Merrill J. Davies describes these difficulties from the perspective of a high school English teacher. Although the honors program in her school claims that its graduates are "guaranteed to be ready for college," Davies tells us, "having taught high school English for thirty-one years, the one thing that I have learned is that there is no guarantee that students who do well in high school composition will automatically do well in college composition." In her effort to balance the uncertainties of college with her school's pledge to guarantee success, Davies explains, "I tell them what I think they should know and be able to do, but in reality I know that the expectations vary greatly between colleges and even among professors in the same college" (31–32). Considering these unpredictable variations within and among schools, what does it mean to be "ready for college"?

Increasingly standardized high school curricula and testing systems attempt to reduce these uncertainties and bridge the divides between diverse high schools and diverse colleges. But these bridges lead only to the gates of higher education: college admissions offices. Standardized classes and examinations cannot prepare students for the richly unstandardized learning environments that lie beyond those gates. When they enter college, students must be prepared, above all, to adapt to these new environments.

For this reason, *The Transition to College Writing* differs from many textbooks that describe general skills and methods for writing college papers. Instead, this book is a guide to adjustment. It explains the interrelated ways in which approaches to writing, reading, and learning most often need to change in undergraduate studies.

Considering the great variety of schools, subjects, learning goals, and teaching methods that equally diverse students encounter in college, the task of writing such a book might be considered "whistling in the dark" as well. In writing, as in other dimensions of academic work, the specific challenges of adjusting to college differ from one student to another for reasons that college teachers, like high school teachers, can't entirely predict or explain.

Among these diverse problems of adjustment, however, there are some underlying patterns that I'll use as foundations for offering specific advice. Standardized preparations for college admissions encourage some common strategies for completing assigned writing, reading, and other work in college. The volume and pace of college work encourages new students to adopt expedient methods to avoid falling behind in their courses from one day or week to the next—methods they typically learn from one another. And there are also recognizable patterns in the ways that these typical approaches to writing and learning are misaligned with the real demands of undergraduate studies and the real expectations of college teachers.

Because these expectations vary, as Merrill Davies observed, standard, all-purpose methods of writing papers or completing assigned readings, for example, cannot be the most effective or efficient methods for all writing and reading. In a pattern that underlies this variation, furthermore, college teachers in all fields value critical thinking, active learning, and intellectual engagement more highly than most undergraduates realize. In other words, common problems of adjustment to college studies often result not from the lack of skills or knowledge but from misunderstandings.

The first two chapters of *The Transition to College Writing* explain the underlying causes of these misunderstandings, some basic differences between high school and college, and the essential connections between language and learning in all fields of study. The example of note taking, in Chapter 2, establishes two central themes for the book:

- Routine, all-purpose methods are rarely the best options for completing college work efficiently and effectively.

- In all facets of their work, the most successful college students use active learning strategies to figure out the best ways to write, read, and learn in particular courses.

Quickly or slowly, with guidance from teachers or through trial and error, all students must make these adjustments, diversifying their approaches to college work and learning *how* to learn in new environments. Subsequent chapters aim to facilitate this process for methods of reading (Chapter 3) and writing (Chapter 4), understanding of rules and errors (Chapter 5), distinct forms of academic writing (Chapter 6), documentation and reference to the work of others (Chapter 7), and the completion of research papers (Chapter 8). In every case, these chapters identify the most common approaches that students initially use in college work, explain their limitations, and describe effective alternatives.

Although I've addressed this advice most directly to students who have recently entered college, it should be useful to students at all stages of the transition to college, from the later years of high school through the first year of college and beyond, when necessary adjustments to writing and learning continue. And although I've tried to make *The Transition to College Writing* continuously readable from beginning to end, it can also be used as a reference to particular aspects of college work as questions and problems arise.

New to the Second Edition

The first edition of a textbook always represents the author's best guesses about what will be most clear and most useful to its readers. With the benefit of valuable advice from students and teachers who used the first edition of *The Transition to College Writing* and from editors at Bedford/ St. Martin's, this second edition has been extensively revised.

As a result of these suggestions, I streamlined and reorganized what was already a brief text to emphasize central principles and recommendations that readers found most helpful. In this second edition, however, I've also added or expanded several sections and included one new chapter, as noted in this list of the most important changes:

- In Chapter 1, new case studies of individual students and a section called "Mythical Colleges, Mythical High Schools" that illustrate why adjustments to college are necessary.

- A new chapter (Chapter 7) called "Writing in Reference to Others," to clarify the basic principles and purposes of reference that are often obscured, in the minds of student writers, by bewilderingly complex rules for documentation.

- More extensive information on documentation systems.

- Expanded discussion of the use of electronic sources and systems in undergraduate writing.

- New examples of readings and of student writing.

- A new section (in Chapter 5) that is addressed to nonnative speakers of English.

- A new concluding chapter, "The Whole Point of Writing," about broad questions of motivation and value in college writing.

- Brief "Guidelines" at the end of each chapter to remind readers of the core principles that the chapter explains in greater detail.

Acknowledgments

Over the past two years, my colleague Elliot Shapiro gave me the opportunity to consult with students who were reading and writing reviews of the first edition in three of his first-year writing seminars. Most recently, Elliot's students Daniel Aguel, Evan Ahn, Jennie Lin, Jacey Pudney, Hyeongsu Park, Ji-heum Park, Sangwon Shin, Tommy Tang, Helen Wang, and Christina Yip posted especially valuable chapter reviews of the first edition on a course Web site, wrote summary reviews at the end of the term, and met with me to discuss their ideas for revision. These students were extremely candid and helpful in telling me what they found the most and the least useful in the text, what they understood and did not understand, and what they read and did not read. And effective reading strategies, they told me, were both essential to writing and more crucial to their studies than I had realized. Elliot's students also persuaded me to move a revised chapter on reading toward the beginning of the book and to add the section on "Mythical Colleges, Mythical High Schools" in Chapter 1.

Although their teachers are academic specialists, undergraduates—especially in the first two years of college—are the truly interdisciplinary members of academic communities. In the lives of college students, therefore, writing and reading are thoroughly interdisciplinary activities, as essential to studies of biology, physics, or sociology as they are to studies of literature, philosophy, or history. In my efforts to represent this breadth and variety in the experiences of undergraduates, I rely on many years of collaboration with faculty members, graduate students, and undergraduates associated with the Knight Institute for Writing in the Disciplines at Cornell University, currently directed by Paul Sawyer. Several teachers in the Knight Institute's programs wrote assignments presented in Chapter 6: William Kennedy (comparative literature), Lynda Bogel (film studies), William Barnett (philosophy), Dan Usner (history), Paul Doremus (political science), David Post (biology), Yervant Terzian (astronomy), and Stanley Marcus (chemistry). My own teaching, writing, and consultations with teachers at other schools have been continually enriched and refreshed by collaboration with my closest colleagues in the Knight Institute: Darlene Evans, Mary Gilliland, Katherine Gottschalk, Barbara LeGendre, Joe Martin, Wendy Martin, Judith Pierpont, and Elliot Shapiro. Three of the student essays quoted in this book were published in issues of *Discoveries*, the Knight Institute's journal of student writing, edited by Joe Martin and Steve Donatelli.

Bedford/St. Martin's primarily develops authors, not just books. This is more or less what Chuck Christensen told me in my first meeting with him, when the ideas that led to this book were still poorly developed. And through many further consultations with Chuck, Joan Feinberg, Karen Henry, and others at Bedford/St. Martin's, this collaborative ordering of means and ends carried me through the complex process that resulted in the first edition of *The Transition to College Writing*. Extremely helpful discussions with Joan Feinberg, Karen Henry, Amy Gershman, and other members of the Bedford/St. Martin's staff carried me through the almost equally complex process of producing this second edition. I'm especially grateful to Marisa Feinstein for her close attention and thoughtful advice on successive drafts of this edition. In this process I also benefited greatly from the comments of many Bedford/St. Martin's sales representatives and from professional reviews provided by John Avery, Green River Community College; Ronit Berger, Rice University; Andrew J. Cavanaugh, University of Maryland University College; Victoria Cliett, Henry Ford Community College; Caroline L. Eisner, University of Michigan; Mary F. Engel, The University of Scranton; Leah B. Glasser, Mount Holyoke College; Gregory R. Glau,

Arizona State University; Laurel Kennedy, Denison University; Emily J. Levitt, Cornell University; Barbara Gaal Lutz, University of Delaware; David Marlow, University of South Carolina, Upstate; Jodi Koslow Martin, Aurora University; Mark D. Merritt, University of San Francisco; Gayla Mills, Randolph-Macon College; Marlene M. Preston, Virginia Tech; Kent Richmond, California State University, Long Beach; Lorraine Hale Robinson, East Carolina University; Kathryn R. Spike, Bowling Green State University; Robert H. Trudeau, Providence College; and Leslie Woodward, Columbia University.

Contents

The Transition to College Writing

1 Orientation

> That burning day when I got ready to leave New York and start out on my journey to college! I felt like Columbus starting out for the other end of the earth. I felt like the pilgrim fathers who had left their homeland and all their kin behind them and trailed out in search of the New World.
>
> —Anzia Yezierska

> To exist is to change, to change is to mature, to mature is to go on creating oneself endlessly.
>
> —Henri Bergson

Are You Prepared for College?

It isn't difficult to understand why Anzia Yezierska experienced a "New World" when she entered Columbia University in 1904. At that time, when high school was still very high on the educational ladder, going to college was a rare opportunity, especially for a young woman born in a Russian Jewish ghetto in Poland and raised in a tenement on the Lower East Side of Manhattan. In 1910, only 2.7 percent of Americans over the age of twenty-five had completed college, most of them from wealthy families in the eastern states, and the average American had completed only eight years of school. Because only about 4 percent of high school graduates continued their education, there were fewer than 1,000 colleges and universities in the United States, with an average enrollment of only 250 undergraduates. To be one of those students was a great privilege, set apart from the ordinary lives of working Americans. "All the young people I had ever seen were shut up in factories," Yezierska recalled in her autobiographical novel *The Bread Givers*. "But here were young girls and young men enjoying life, free from the worry for a living."

1

More remarkable, considering the dramatic changes over the past century, is the fact that most undergraduates still experience college as a new world, both exciting and confusing, filled with unexpected opportunities and challenges. If you are entering college this year, you represent the majority, about 63 percent, of high school graduates nationwide. Each fall more than 3 million high school graduates begin their studies at more than 4,000 American colleges and universities, with an average enrollment of 3,900 students. Nearly 17 million students are currently enrolled in undergraduate or graduate programs in the United States. What was once a rare privilege has become a statistical norm and, for many careers, a necessity.

With the expansion of college enrollments, high schools, in coordination with testing services and college admissions offices, have raised the priority of preparing their students for this transition. In high school, many of you have taken honors or advanced placement courses designed to prepare you for undergraduate studies. You have taken batteries of standardized tests, perhaps two or three times, possibly with the help of coaching services. Parents, friends, teachers, and guidance counselors may have helped you to identify the schools that correspond with your interests, credentials, and financial resources. Published guides to colleges, catalogues and brochures, detailed Web sites, and campus visits provide additional views of undergraduate life at particular schools. Each year, millions of high school seniors and graduates enter a complex matchmaking system with college admissions officers, who review applications filled with detailed aptitude and achievement scores, Advanced Placement (AP) scores, high school transcripts, class ranks, lists of honors and activities, personal essays, and letters of recommendation.

For the purpose of orchestrating admission to college, this matchmaking system works remarkably well. In its survey of students who entered four-year colleges in the fall of 2004, *The Chronicle of Higher Education* found that more than 90 percent were attending their first or second choice of schools. From this limited perspective, we might imagine that going to college has become an ordinary, predictable experience, effectively regulated by educators at both ends of a transition that has become straight and smooth.

But research and experience tell a different story. For a great variety of reasons, 35 percent of first-year students discontinue their studies, at least temporarily, by the beginning of the sophomore year; according to current projections, only 54 percent will graduate within the next six years. And college teachers still complain, as they have for more than a century, that their students are unprepared for the kinds of writing, reading, thinking, and learning required in undergraduate studies.

Students who are entering college obviously run into a variety of obstacles they did not anticipate, and high school credentials, furthermore, cannot reliably predict a student's performance in college, especially in the first year. Students with weak high school backgrounds often do extremely well; those with superb credentials sometimes have the most difficulty adjusting to undergraduate studies. For reasons we will explore throughout this book, even the most thorough preparations for college differ from the real experiences and challenges of *being* a college student. As a consequence, strategies for success in high school and in college admissions are not reliable prescriptions for success in undergraduate courses.

Examples of two of my students will illustrate some of the unpredictable factors that determine whether individuals will adapt quickly or slowly, successfully or unsuccessfully, to the new challenges of college work.

Eduardo and Marie

In their first semester of college, Eduardo and Marie were both enrolled in a writing seminar I taught. Admitted to college as a "disadvantaged minority" student, Eduardo was raised in a dangerous, impoverished urban neighborhood and attended a public high school that sent a low percentage of its students to college. His mother, a single parent, had little formal education and spoke to her children in Spanish, her native language, and Eduardo's verbal test scores were somewhat low. Marie, by contrast, came from a wealthy suburban family and attended an exclusive private high school, designed to prepare students for admission to competitive colleges and universities. There, she had performed well in Advanced Placement courses, and her test scores were high, especially in math and science.

At the end of that first semester, Eduardo had adapted to college studies with apparent ease and obvious success. Without any of the typical signs of exhaustion or stress, he had achieved a perfect 4.0 (A) average for the term. Marie, however, had struggled to complete the term with a C average, even though she devoted enormous amounts of time to her courses. After studying all night, trying to memorize the course material, she failed her first examination of the semester, in physics. Concluding that she needed to work harder, she became increasingly tired and distressed.

Due in part to her struggles in her other courses, in response to assignments in my writing class, Marie relied on simple formulas she had learned in high school (formulas I'll discuss further in Chapter 6). And although the resulting essays were orderly and correct, they often missed the point of the assignment and shed little light on the subject. Eduardo spent less time on his papers, I suspect, yet his work was always thoughtful and interesting to read in ways that captured the specific and changing purposes of my assignments.

I should note that the ends of these stories are both happy. Because the first year of college is a period of transition and adjustment, the unpredictable factors that influence student performance in that year extend to the following years as well. In later semesters, Marie gradually figured out how to complete her work more effectively, and when she graduated and entered a master's program in engineering, she was an excellent student. Eduardo continued to refine his learning skills and graduated with a nearly perfect record in economics. In the beginning, however, their strategies for adapting to college work were dramatically different, in ways that all students may find instructive.

Because Eduardo's transition to college was extraordinarily smooth and effective, I asked him to explain how he got all of his work done so efficiently, with such reliable success. His answer suggested a remarkable combination of alertness and flexibility, along with a strong sense of opportunity and enjoyment in learning. "I think that every course, every assignment, is a different little puzzle I have to solve," he explained. "What do I need to do here? When do I need to do it, and how long will it take? What does this teacher expect from me?"

Although he certainly made good use of the knowledge and skills he brought with him to college, Eduardo didn't confuse his classes in college with those in high school, even when they were in the same subject. Nor did he confuse his college classes and assignments with one another. Although he could observe real similarities and connections that gradually made learning increasingly efficient, he never assumed that *reading, writing, studying,* or *being a good student* had the same meanings in different courses or assignments. When writing a paper for me, he could figure out what *I* wanted him to do, partly because he didn't confuse my expectations with those of his high school English teachers or his current sociology or economics teachers. Then he figured out how much time he could reasonably spend on this assignment, considering his other responsibilities, and he scheduled that time accordingly.

During Marie's first semester, her approach to college work seemed to run on a kind of automatic pilot, set by a few basic assumptions she had brought to college, such as *"Work hard and you will do well"* or *"Learning is remembering what teachers and textbooks say."*

Following such premises, if you work hard but *don't* do well, the only recourse is to work harder to do better. Although Eduardo always considered the advantages of working *differently*, or even *less*, Marie could only imagine working *more*. In turn, *studying*, for Marie, primarily meant *reading*, and the main goal of reading was *memorization*. While this generic approach to learning had worked well enough in most of her high school classes, especially in math and science, it did not work reliably in college, for reasons we will explore further in this book. Her physics course, for example, had quickly covered too much information for her to remember, and the exam questions required "understanding" or "application" of the main concepts. This also required *thinking*. Filled with a jumble of information from a sleepless night of cramming for a different kind of examination, her brain could not think about the questions at all. Although Marie was a capable writer, she approached writing assignments with similar inflexibility, allowing formulas that had worked in the past to override her attention to the specific demands of writing in the present.

Eduardo and Marie seemed to be equally bright, capable students, and I can't explain the different approaches with which they began their college studies. I don't know, for example, how Eduardo developed such acutely adaptive skills, beyond the fact that he had to contend with many unpredictable, potentially hazardous situations at home and at school.

But I do know that Marie had to develop—and was able to develop—the same kinds of skills to succeed in college. And for reasons I will explain, all successful college students must develop these flexible strategies for writing and learning in changing environments.

Mythical Colleges, Mythical High Schools

Why are these adjustments necessary? What prevents students like Marie from recognizing that college work requires new learning strategies? And why do college teachers often fail to explain the particular ways in which entering students need to adapt to their expectations?

Here I'll answer these questions in very general terms, with the help of simple diagrams, and in the following section I'll explain the basic differences between high school and college that make new approaches to learning essential.

The fact that college represents a turning point in students' lives shouldn't surprise anyone. Colleges and universities advertise the new experiences and opportunities they offer to students as main attractions, and few of you would either expect or want this experience to be a direct, routine continuation of high school. Higher education has always offered people the opportunity to reinvent themselves and find new directions for their lives among diverse options that weren't open to them in the past. Beyond this turning point, much of the knowledge and skill you previously acquired will remain useful, but the credentials that brought you to this point will suddenly become irrelevant. When college admissions officers close your application folder and put it in the ACCEPTANCE pile, I doubt that anyone will ever look at your high school record again. Previous triumphs, struggles, and failures are in this sense erased, and what you do from now on is all that matters.

Freshman orientation and advising programs introduce new students to unfamiliar social, administrative, and practical features of campus life. As a rule, entering students receive lots of help in meeting one another, settling into dorms or other housing, registering for classes, learning about campus organizations, and coping with other bewildering details of living in a new place.

Orientations to intellectual life and to new ways of learning are more difficult to provide, and the need for change in these areas is easier to ignore. One reason is that increasingly standardized systems that lead to college admissions create illusions of academic continuity between high school and college. Although living in a new social and physical environment may be disorienting in every other way, the measured skills that got students into a particular school seem to represent a solid bridge and clear path to further success. Lacking obvious alternatives, students will tend to stay on this path as long as they can. And when it leads them into trouble, they may conclude, as Marie did, that college work simply requires *more effort*, not *different kinds of effort*, for different purposes.

Failing to recognize that admission to college is a dramatic turning point in learning, as in other aspects of their lives, undergraduates often approach their studies as though they were attending a mythical college or university: the kind of school for which they are already prepared to succeed, without substantial changes. Students like Marie therefore seem unprepared for college because they imagine that they *are* prepared. The diagram shown below illustrates this straight path that students often try to follow, along with the dramatic turn they must take to contend with the realities of undergraduate studies successfully.

In the next section I'll explain why high school teachers cannot reliably predict the expectations that students will actually encounter when they make this turn into specific courses and fields of study at particular schools. But these expectations would not remain mysterious if all college teachers clearly explained the changes they expected students to make in writing papers, reading assigned texts, taking notes, participating in discussions, or studying for exams. Why do individual teachers fail to make their expectations clear to students?

To varying degrees, professors do provide instructions and guidance for completing assignments and other work for their courses. They specify the lengths and usually the forms of assigned papers or

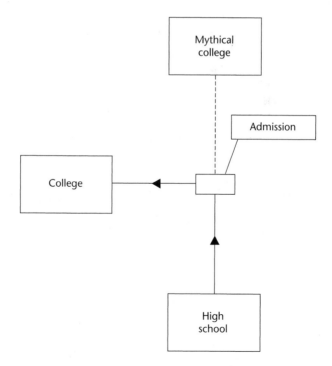

the questions they want students to consider while writing or reading. They also describe the forms of impending examinations and may offer hints about coverage and strategies for studying. But these guidelines rarely include explanations of the particular ways you should write papers, read assigned texts, or learn about the subject; and they are even less likely to describe the ways in which you must adapt to this work, in moving from high school to college or from one college class to another. To illustrate why the real expectations of college teachers remain bewildering, therefore, we must add another vector to our diagram shown below.

You probably wouldn't conclude on your own that the failure of college teachers to explain what they expect results from ignorance. As teachers in their own areas of expertise, professors may seem omniscient. If their standards are difficult to understand and more difficult to meet, the most obvious explanation is that they know so much more than you do. In their roles as teachers, however, there is one important area they know very little about: the academic backgrounds, skills, and learning strategies that you bring to college and to their particular courses.

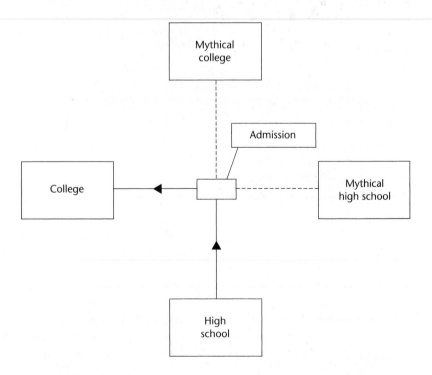

From the perspectives of college teachers, the real high schools you attended also lie beyond a corner they can't see around, in environments they can't reliably imagine. And much in the way that entering students envision a mythical learning environment as the logical extension of their preparations for college, professors often imagine mythical high schools as the logical extensions of everything students should have learned in preparation for college work. "Don't they teach that in high school?" they often ask.

Because they think these mythical high schools should be responsible for teaching students the kinds of writing, reading, logical reasoning, critical thinking, and other skills required in undergraduate classes, college teachers will tend to assume that you are already familiar with these expectations or that you will make the necessary adjustments on your own. And because most of these teachers know very little about high school instruction, even in their own fields, they could not clearly describe necessary changes in your approaches to learning even if they felt responsible for doing so.

Illusions of continuity between high school and college therefore persist on both sides of the admissions process, in the minds of college students and of college teachers. For the purpose of negotiating the real *discontinuities* between these environments, however, you hold the clear advantage. Unlike your college teachers, you know what you actually learned in high school, along with the writing, reading, and learning strategies you bring to college work. At this turning point, you can see in both directions and, with a clear eye and open mind, observe the differences.

Some Basic Differences between High School and College

I've argued that even the best high schools can fully prepare you only for *admission* to college. High school teachers can't accurately predict your college experience, and college teachers can't reliably imagine your high school background because high schools, colleges, and the transitions between any two of them are actually quite diverse.

High schools vary greatly in size—from fewer than a hundred students in some rural and private schools to urban and suburban districts with enrollments of several thousand. But variations in higher education are even more extreme. Among the 4,236 colleges and universities in the United States, about 450, more than 10 percent, enroll fewer than 200 students. At the opposite end of the scale, 166 universities are at least 100 times larger, enrolling 20,000 to 50,000 students at a single campus. As a consequence, some of you might go to colleges that are smaller than your high schools, whereas others enroll in universities that are larger than the towns in which you were raised. About 80 percent of you will attend colleges in your home states, and some of you will travel only a few miles from your homes, where you might continue to live. Others will cross the entire continent or arrive from other countries, moving from large cities to small towns or from rural areas to urban centers. College tuition varies radically as well, and so do standards for admission, curricula, housing, physical and social environments, and patterns of diversity in the student body.

The many differences among colleges and universities were no doubt important factors in your choice of schools. They also determine the particular adjustments you have to make as individuals, entering college with different backgrounds. Across these variations, however, some basic, categorical differences exist between high school and college, to which most of you must adapt. These factors represent foundations for particular kinds of writing, reading, and learning that will be discussed in later chapters.

College courses are not direct continuations of high school instruction.   As I noted, standardized tests create illusions of uniformity and continuity, partly because many of the high school courses billed as preparation for college studies actually prepare students to pass the standardized exams that are essential for college admissions. In some basic subjects, these classes do provide excellent foundations for introductory college courses. A good high school calculus or precalculus class will be a great asset to you in your first year of college mathematics and science. The same will be true for good high school courses in chemistry, biology, physics, and computer science. The periodic table, the principles of genetics, and the laws of motion aren't likely to change between your senior year of high school and the first year of college. Nor are the dates of important historical events, or the structures and vocabularies of English, French, or Spanish.

Even in these basic subjects, however, methods of instruction and evaluation will vary considerably. Freshman courses in English literature, psychology, American history, or philosophy will not necessarily cover the material you studied in high school versions of these courses, nor will they proceed with the same assumptions about what is important and true.

In addition, many of the subjects you study in college do not exist in the high school curriculum. The average university encompasses about fifty academic departments and interdisciplinary programs, each with its own faculty, roster of courses, prerequisites, and requirements for undergraduate majors. At the freshman level in the social sciences, for example, introductory courses often represent branches of study within these departments: microeconomics, international politics, cultural anthropology, social psychology, or the sociology of religion.

While high school teachers are usually generalists, college teachers are specialists. Your college professors will not directly coordinate their courses with high school instruction because most of them know very little about the high school curriculum. Professors who teach introductory courses in their departments are specialists in certain types of research. They are not just biologists but are particular types of molecular biologists, neurobiologists, or geneticists; they are not just historians but are specialists on particular periods and features of English, American, Brazilian, or West African history. These teachers view introductory courses not as extensions of high school but as points of departure into advanced studies.

Principles of "academic freedom" encourage variation in college teaching. "Academic freedom" means that within broad guidelines for fairness and responsibility, individual college professors are free to decide what and how they should teach. College courses are rarely governed by the kinds of state and local mandates that standardize secondary education, and most college professors are not required to pass through formal teacher training and certification. As a consequence, two professors in the same political science department, for example, may teach an introduction to political theory with very different course designs, texts, assignments, and examinations. One might emphasize factual knowledge, through formal lectures and short-answer exams. The other might emphasize critical thinking and lead discussion-based classes, assigning position papers and a research project in place of exams.

This variation is most dramatic in the first year. In your first year or two, most of your courses will satisfy degree requirements that are designed to ensure broad exposure to the sciences, social sciences, and humanities. In a single day, therefore, you might travel from a large lecture course in chemistry to a writing class that is taught as a seminar or workshop, and then to a small lecture course in cognitive psychology that includes student participation and to a biology lab where you work on experiments with a partner. Your friends, meanwhile, are probably taking other courses of diverse sizes and designs in other departments—in anthropology, education, philosophy, astronomy, nutrition, or calculus. The following semester you will take different courses, some of them in other departments, with teachers who have their own unpredictable ideas about what and how you should learn. At large schools, especially, individual professors will have little or no idea what you are doing (or how much you have to do) in other courses.

College work requires new kinds of motivation and self-discipline. In their first year, most of my students face the necessity of finding new reasons for getting their work done and new ways of making productive use of their time among many potential distractions. When they were in high school, their parents, teachers, and school officials often made sure they were attending classes, completing assignments, and meeting requirements from one day or week to the next. In high school, they also worked hard for the purpose of getting into college.

In college, most of those structured expectations vanish. On any particular day you will be free to skip class, postpone work on assignments, and spend your time in many other tempting ways. Because colleges give students much greater freedom and responsibility, they can easily fall behind in their work, sometimes even to the point of failing classes, without any intervention from their teachers. Problems with time management and motivation account for a large proportion of the students who leave college in their first year, including some who were very successful in high school. For this reason, the most successful college students deliberately reconsider their motivations and make thoughtful decisions about the use of their time.

Take Charge of Your Own Transition to College, as Active Learners

Many students seem to drift through the first year of college, and sometimes through later years as well, letting immediate circumstances structure their time and priorities from one hour or day to the next. In some cases, frequent distractions divert their attention from work they need to be doing. As deadlines loom, the resulting scramble to complete readings, papers, and other assignments greatly reduces effectiveness, engagement, and pleasure in their academic work. At best, these students drift into a more or less functional routine of attending classes and completing assignments, without evaluating their motives and methods. Without considering why they are doing this work, beyond a vague sense of obligation or a fear of bad grades, they attend college as though it were an advanced version of high school: another level of compulsory education. The real, transformative opportunities of college are thus diminished, if not altogether lost.

Successful college students find internal motivations and discipline to replace the external factors that may have kept them focused in high school. These students tell me that they do not want to disappoint themselves or waste opportunities, and that they take pride in learning to be both independent and responsible—to achieve their own goals. They insist that they are not working just to meet course requirements and get high grades, which they view as a *result* of their motivations, not as motivations in themselves. *In other words, students who get the most out of college usually take the most active responsibility for determining what, how, and why they should learn.*

The great importance of active learning became clearer to me a few years ago when I interviewed a group of seniors chosen to participate in a fellowship program for the most promising biology majors. I hoped to identify the approaches to college studies that contributed to their success, and I was asking these questions on behalf of capable students at lower levels, such as Marie, who were running into trouble in their courses, even when they worked very hard. In our discussion, I was surprised to learn that in their first year most of these students had elected to take the "autotutorial" course in introductory biology, rather than the conventional lecture/laboratory courses designed for science majors. "Why did you choose that course?" I asked. "It's just the best way to learn," one of them said. "In reality, all of our courses are autotutorial." Others smiled and nodded in agreement, but I wasn't sure what he meant. "If you think you can understand the material just by putting in your time, listening to lectures, and doing the assigned readings," he explained, "you won't do very well. If you really want to understand the subject, you always have to get interested in it for your own reasons, and teach yourself." Another student added, "And teach each other."

These students explained that they usually studied together, in pairs or small groups, and educational research supports their belief that, for the purpose of learning, "two heads are better than one." Here are some other active learning strategies these students had chosen:

- Whenever possible, they chose smaller classes in which they could develop and communicate their understanding in writing, discussion, and presentations. They preferred these learning environments to impersonal lecture courses with formal examinations.

- They avoided procrastination, completing readings and starting assigned papers early, so they could participate in class discussions and ask questions about points of confusion.

- For the same purposes, they often talked with teachers after class and during office hours.

- They had taken the initiative to find positions as research assistants to teachers in their fields, or in laboratories, libraries, or other facilities related to their majors.

- They had initiated or joined student organizations in their areas of interest—for example, undergraduate research and study groups, student curriculum committees in their departments, or advocacy groups on particular issues.

In comparison with more passive approaches to learning in college, such active strategies do not necessarily require more time, but they do require thoughtful, deliberate time management. You cannot participate effectively in class discussions or do well in interactive classes, for example, if you haven't found time to complete readings and think about discussion topics in advance. And you can't get help with papers and other assigned projects if you start them the night before they are due.

And well-managed time is something you must deliberately *find*, or create, in your schedule. It won't just be there when you need it. If you are taking a reasonable number of credits, your academic work shouldn't require overwhelming amounts of time each week. On average, college students spend about four hours in class each day and another three hours on out-of-class study and assignments—less, if anything, than a full-time job. But this time is not so neatly blocked into work hours. With complex academic schedules, irregular workloads throughout the term, many extracurricular events, membership in campus organizations, constant opportunities for social activity, and often part-time jobs and athletic practices all competing for their time and attention, college students tend to lead hectic, fragmented lives. Scheduling all of this activity effectively is a complicated task that, in itself, requires constant attention.

- For this reason, one of your first purchases in college should be a good "academic planner," or "daybook," with enough space for each day to list everything you need to do. An electronic notebook that you can always carry with you will serve the same purpose. At the beginning of each term, enter all of your regular class times and (from the syllabi for your courses) all of the scheduled times for exams, due dates for papers, and other assigned work, along with work hours (if you have a part-time job) and other regular responsibilities. This will give you a sense for the blocks of time available for studying and working on course assignments.

- Revise this schedule on a daily basis, entering new and altered commitments. When papers and other projects are assigned well in advance, note when you should *begin* to work on these projects, not just when they are due.

- With these responsibilities in mind, plan your week in advance, scheduling blocks of time for writing, reading, and other work out of class. Avoid postponing all of your writing and study time until late in the evening, when you are sleepy and exhausted. Nocturnal writing habits account for a lot of the unfocused and unfinished writing that students turn in.

In a book about writing, I offer this general advice about time management because the quality of your written work will depend heavily on the time and attention you can devote to it in a typically complex and busy schedule.

GUIDELINES

- Because college remains a transformative experience, high schools can fully prepare students only for *admission* to college, not for the challenges of *being* a college student.

- Because the expectations of college teachers may vary unpredictably, meeting these challenges requires both alertness and flexibility. In the first year, especially, view every assignment in every course as a puzzle you must solve.

- In each of these contexts, ask yourself what it means, exactly, for you to *read, write, study,* or *be a good student.*

- These flexible adjustments are necessary because colleges differ from high schools in some fundamental ways (pp. 9–12).

- For all of the preceding reasons, the most successful students take active responsibility for their own learning and for the thoughtful management of their time.

2 Language and Learning

> The foundation for a successful undergraduate experience is proficiency in the written and the spoken word. Students need language to grasp and express effectively feelings and ideas. To succeed in college, undergraduates should be able to write and speak with clarity, and to read and listen with comprehension. Language and thought are inextricably connected, and as undergraduates develop their linguistic skills, they hone the quality of their thinking and become intellectually and socially empowered.
>
> —Ernest Boyer, *The Undergraduate Experience in America*

The Vital Connections between Language and Learning

To examine the complex and changing roles of writing in higher education, we should begin with a broad view of writing among other, related uses of language. On the basis of prior experience, you may associate writing skills with the production of assigned essays, primarily in subjects such as English or history. Among all uses of written language, however, formal papers or reports will represent only a fraction of the writing you do in college, and these diverse forms of writing are linked with other uses of language that are just as crucial to learning.

In every type of course, in every department, language is the primary medium of teaching and learning. Some classes also rely on other media: visual representations (such as pictures, diagrams, and films), demonstrations, hands-on activities (such as lab experiments), or mathematics. But about 90 percent of instruction in college is verbal, and the ways you use language as a student—as a writer, reader, speaker, and listener—will largely determine your levels of performance in all of your courses.

Several years ago, a Korean student helped me to realize the overwhelming importance of language in education. As a college freshman, Linda told me that when she moved to the United States and entered the sixth grade, she spoke and understood only a few words of English. Her suburban school had no English as a Second Language program, and none of the students and teachers spoke Korean. Other students were assigned to escort her to classes, but when she got to the classroom, she had no idea what was going on.

- She couldn't understand what the teachers and students were saying.
- She was unable to read textbooks, assignments, or writing on the chalkboard.
- She didn't know how to take notes or do homework assignments.
- She wasn't able to ask questions or get help from other students in her classes.
- She couldn't figure out how much she knew or didn't know in particular subjects—whether she belonged in the sixth grade or, as she often felt, back in kindergarten.

"I felt completely stupid and helpless," Linda told me, "until I got to math class."

In that class, the teacher put a math problem on the board and stood back, speaking to the students as though he were asking them to solve it. With enormous relief, Linda realized she had learned to do this kind of problem two years earlier in Korea. To demonstrate to everyone that she had a mind that worked, she walked straight to the board, solved the problem, and returned to her desk. The teacher nodded and smiled with approval. Other students smiled at her, too, and looked impressed. That moment gave Linda confidence—for the first time—that she was smart enough to survive in this country. Mathematics was a language she knew. And in this foreign place, becoming a good student meant learning to use English just as well.

In its diverse forms, language was no less essential to learning when Linda was attending school in Korea, using her native language. It was no less important for her fellow students in the United States, and it is no less important for you, whether English is your native language or not. In familiar situations, however, we take most of these uses of language for granted or call them by other names:

- Paying attention in class
- Taking notes
- Studying
- Doing homework
- Taking exams
- Asking questions
- Participating in discussions
- Getting help

In every type of class, you are engaged in some or all of these linguistic activities, along with more obvious uses of language such as writing papers. In every course you take, the ways teachers and students use language determine the kinds of instruction and learning that will occur. Even in her mathematics class, Linda could not learn new material easily until she could understand what her teacher was saying, read explanations in her textbook, and ask questions.

In recent years, furthermore, these uses of language have become more diverse and interconnected in ways that blur the boundaries between writing and speech or between visual and textual media. Many of your courses will have web pages with links to other Web sites and assigned texts, audio files, or images available in electronic forms. Some courses will hold discussions beyond the classroom, in class e-mail lists or blogs. In ways we will examine in Chapter 8, "research" has also become an increasingly electronic enterprise, through the wealth of resources on the Internet and through online library systems. Electronic media such as e-mail and text messages share some of the informality and spontaneity of conversational speech.

If you consider all uses of language, therefore, you can analyze what is happening in and around your courses, how their designs and expectations differ, and what it means to become a good student in each of them. In each case, who is speaking, listening, writing, and reading? What forms do these uses of language take?

In a large lecture course, for example, the professor speaks, writes on the board, or uses computer projections, sometimes distributing course descriptions, assignments, and other written material. Comparable information may be available on a course Web site. In class, students usually listen and watch in silence, read the information on the board and in handouts, and write in their notebooks or on laptop computers. Outside class, they do assigned readings, discuss the course with one another, exchange electronic messages, and complete written assignments such as papers, problem sets, and other homework. Prior to exams they read over their course notes, review assigned texts, and perhaps study together. During most exams they are also reading and writing, completing short answers or essay questions to demonstrate what they have learned.

In laboratories, discussion sections, or seminars, learning usually requires more active uses of language from students. They might speak in class while teachers listen, read drafts of other students' papers, work with others in collaborative projects, follow instructions in a lab manual, or give oral presentations with visual projections. In every case, however, learning occurs through forms of linguistic exchange.

Even in the comparatively passive setting of a large lecture class, furthermore, being engaged in these activities can take many forms, and some ways are more effective than others. In later years of college, for example, students often spend less time studying for their courses but with better results because, like Eduardo, they have discovered specific approaches to learning that are most efficient for particular kinds of courses, assignments, and exams. Becoming a better student will often follow the realization that the *amount* of time you spend on your studies can be less important than *how* you spend that time.

In later chapters, we'll see some of the distinct ways of writing and reading for different purposes. Here we'll examine variations in one important type of writing that you will all be required to do at one time or another, even though you may not consider it a writing skill.

Consider Note Taking

During a lecture, almost everyone is taking notes in some form. But are these students actually doing the same thing?

They are not, as a painful experience in my first year of college reminds me. At my assigned seat in the required Western Civilization class, I was listening to an unbroken stream of historical information and trying to figure out what I should write in my notebook. I couldn't record everything the professor was saying, and when I tried to do so,

I fell behind and lost track of his lecture. Finding no solution to the problem, I occasionally wrote something down, more or less at random, in an anxious scrawl.

In the seat next to me, a sophomore listened to these lectures attentively and at the same time calmly produced detailed outlines, in green ink and tidy print. One day she turned to me and said, in a not entirely convincing tone of admiration, "I think it's *amazing* that you can remember all this information with so few notes. I need to write down almost everything, or I'll forget it."

I don't need to tell you who got an A in the course and who got a C–. The notes I took in class were almost useless when I tried to study for the essay exams, which asked us to explain the roles of historical figures, the causes of wars, and the connections among events. My notebooks resembled the ones Mike Rose rediscovered from his first "disengaged and half-awake" semester at Loyola University and that he described in his book *Lives on the Boundary*:

> The one from English is a small book, eight by seven, and only eleven pages of it are filled. The notes I did write consist of book titles, dates of publication, names of characters, pointless summaries of books that were not on our syllabus and that I had never read . . . and quotations from the teacher ("Perception can bring sorrow"). The notes are a series of separate entries. I can't see any coherence. My biology lab notes are written on green-tint quadrille. They, too, are sparse. There is an occasional poorly executed sketch of a tiny organism or of a bone and muscle structure. Some of the formulas and molecular models sit isolated on the page, bare of any explanatory discussion. The lecture notes are fragmented; a fair number of sentences remain incomplete. (42)

Rose eventually became a professor of English at UCLA, but by the end of his second semester of college, he was heading toward academic probation. So was I. What were we doing wrong? What and how did we change?

If you think of note taking as a kind of writing—a use of written language—you can more easily understand and resolve some of the problems that first-year students commonly encounter in lecture courses, and you can understand these problems not as matters of intelligence and capability but as questions of strategy.

The central problem is that note taking forces you to do at least two things at once: *listen* and *write*. Sometimes you also need to *read* information on the board or screen or on handouts. If you use note taking to record everything the teacher says, you will soon fall behind, and in your struggle to catch up, you will miss substantial portions of the lecture, including important connections. For this reason, stenography—trying to write down *everything*—is a lost cause. Listening and writing will be at odds.

Fortunately, you don't have to record everything. Instead, you need to take notes on the most important points and the connections between them to help you reconstruct an understanding of the lecture material a week or a month later. For this purpose, you need to give listening priority over writing: *to put writing in the service of listening, understanding, and remembering.*

The best teachers make this process fairly easy by delivering well-organized lectures at a reasonable pace and using the chalkboard or projections to outline, emphasize, or illustrate important material. Some professors even distribute lecture notes in advance or post them on a Web site so their students can listen and think with full attention. Others, like my Western Civilization professor, deliver masses of information at a rapid pace, without pauses or visual aids. In this kind of class, especially, the following suggestions from some of the most successful undergraduates will be useful.

Do assigned readings before the lecture, not after.   When professors assign readings for particular topics on the course syllabus, they are assuming that you will come to the lectures that week with this background knowledge of the subject. Research on learning indicates that relevant background knowledge greatly increases our ability to make sense of and remember new information. If you have completed reading assignments in advance, therefore, you will find it much easier to understand and take notes on the lectures. If lectures correspond closely with assigned texts, you will also need to take fewer notes when you recognize material available in the readings.

Listen for the structure of the lecture.   This is what my classmate was doing as she calmly produced those neat outlines in her notebook. While I was struggling to record whole sentences verbatim, without knowing why, she was often looking up at the teacher, listening for central themes, subtopics, lists of examples, or causes. At the end of the period, she left with a frame of reference for understanding and remembering the lecture and for correlating the lecture with readings.

(See the example on pp. 24–25.) I, however, left with fragmented bits of stenography that made very little sense a week later.

Fill in details and perspectives shortly after the lecture. For reasons I'll explain in the next chapter, your memory of a lecture will fade very quickly, even if you feel that you understand everything at the end of a class. Because what you wrote down will be about all you have later, at your first break after a class, read over your notes and fill in missing details, observations, and connections. Conscientious students often say they "recopy" their notes shortly after a lecture, but they are really doing more: reorganizing, clarifying, adding information they didn't have time to record, and noting questions they need to resolve.

Adapt your note-taking strategies to the type and design of the course. In my freshman year, my course notebooks looked very similar: all of them filled with clumps of scrawled quotations from the lecture itself, broken occasionally by diagrams I copied from the board. In later, more successful years, my methods varied a lot from one course to another. If exams were based heavily on *information* in lectures, I took extensive notes and reviewed them to make sure they were complete. In courses that required essays based on the *interpretation* of issues, I spent more time listening and thinking about the discussion, paraphrasing central arguments, and noting questions or references for further reading. Occasionally I took no notes at all, or I spent the time recording my own ideas in response to an issue.

Keep "double-entry" notes for some courses. If courses include assigned papers, essay exams, discussion sections, debates, or student presentations, remembering what teachers and readings said will not be sufficient preparation for meeting course requirements. What you have to say *about* readings and issues will be equally important. For this reason, some teachers will ask you to use separate notebooks, sometimes called "reflective journals," in which you record your own thoughts, questions, and evaluations of readings and other course material. This informal writing enriches learning and provides a repository of ideas you can bring to formal writing assignments, discussions, and essay exam questions.

"Double-entry" notes offer similar advantages. On one page of the notebook, you summarize lectures or readings for the purpose of remembering what teachers or authors said. On the opposite page, you record your own thoughts about this material, including questions, critical responses, alternative explanations, or points of particular interest to you for further consideration. When you begin to work on a paper or enter discussions, for example, review of these reflections will give you a basis for presenting your own ideas; your work will then be more thoughtful, engaging, and connected with central issues in the class.

If their reflections accompany lecture notes, students usually fill in or elaborate the reflective sides of these notebooks after the lecture, because keeping summary notes leaves little time for further writing. While reading, however, you will have time to record thoughts as they occur to you, and you can make further observations when you have finished the text. Do this work when your memory is still fresh. Although it will seem to take additional time, these reflections can save time and improve the quality of your work later on. In many courses your thoughts about the topics will be more important than your ability to repeat what you were told.

Following are some examples of "double-entry" notes taken for part of a lecture on the "Digital Divide," in a course on the history of computer technology. In her lecture notes, the student has avoided "stenography" and listened for the structure of the lecture, as recommended previously, recording central concepts and factual information in ways she can easily understand and use later on. On the "reflective" side, she noted the first, general question that occurred to her during the lecture (about the real lines of the "Divide") and expanded on this question shortly after class. These questions and ideas of her own will be very useful to her for completing essay exam questions and assigned papers that emphasize critical and analytical thinking about the topics.

Lecture Notes

"Digital Divide"

Termed in 1980s and 1990s (also as "knowledge gap" or "computer literacy")

Distinguishes "have" and "have-not" nations

Ex.:	African nations	14% of world pop.
		1.7% of Internet users
	North Am.	5.1% of world pop.
		23.8% of Int. users
	South Asia	6.8 computers/1,000 people
	Europe	317.2 " " "

In 2000, 82% of Web content in English

"Divide" roughly correlates with GDP: 24 times lower in low-income countries.

Competing theories: Divide caused by
1. access (infrastructure)
2. skills/literacy (users)

Reflective Notes

Where are the real dividing lines exactly? Between nations or within nations? Are they socioeconomic or technological, political, educational?

And is the correlation just the amount of wealth or the distribution of wealth and power? Ex.: Gov. control of Internet in Burma. Does dist. of wealth correlate with dist. of computer access?

In theory, you could have high GDP and low access due to hoarding by small elite (Nigeria?) or low GDP and even distribution w/ public access to technology.

Is this a "divide" or a jigsaw puzzle?

Review your notes with friends in the class.   These review sessions have two main functions. Friends might have noted important information or connections that you missed, or they might have understood the material from a different, valuable perspective. Research on note taking suggests that on the average, individual students write down only about 35 percent of important information. In the process of explaining this material to each other, you will grasp more; the exchange will also strengthen both your understanding and your memory.

Forms and Functions of a College Writing Class ___

Entering students have always had trouble adapting to the unfamiliar standards for writing and reading in higher education. When Harvard began to use entrance examinations for writing skills in 1874, more than half of the entering freshmen failed the exam. This weak performance led to the first required writing courses for students at Harvard, and other schools soon adopted similar courses and requirements. Today, the majority of colleges and universities in the United States require students to take at least one class on writing (perhaps called composition or communication) in their first year. Many schools also require at least one advanced course that emphasizes writing and other communication skills.

More than any other type of course or requirement in undergraduate studies, first-year writing classes address the transition between high school and college and prepare students for the purposes of general education: to help you write, read, and think more effectively in all of your courses. Because writing classes serve these general purposes and are usually offered through departments of English, it's easy to think of them as extensions of the English instruction typically required throughout the years of high school. From this narrow perspective (also rooted in the first entrance exams at Harvard), college writing instruction seems *remedial*—designed to fill gaps or repair weaknesses in language skills that high schools should have assembled. Completing these requirements will then appear to certify that you have the skills you need for further writing in college and that you shouldn't have to take "writing" (or English or composition) again.

But this popular "inoculation" theory of writing skills is seriously flawed and undermines the potential benefits of writing instruction in the first year of college and beyond. Most advanced students and their teachers will testify that they have never finished learning how to communicate, in writing or in other forms. Instead, writing becomes increasingly complex, specialized, and in some ways difficult in every field of study and career, even for experienced writers. In this respect, a first-year writing course is not the end of a learning process that began in primary school and continued through high school. It is, like the first year of college, the new beginning of a learning process that will continue throughout your life.

College writing teachers understand, perhaps more than anyone, that they can't teach in just one or two courses *everything* you need to know to use language effectively in all of your courses and careers. Because the challenges of using language well are so diverse and complex, writing teachers have to choose a limited range of priorities for emphasis.

For this reason, writing classes and programs vary considerably from one school to another. Although most general, first-year composition classes are offered in English, they typically do not focus on reading and writing about works of literature such as stories and novels. Instead, these general English composition courses tend to emphasize the development of arguments, comparisons, critical analyses, or reflective essays based on topics and readings on diverse subjects. They are also likely to help you to master the use and documentation of sources, with orientation to the large and complex library resources available to college students.

In recent years, however, many college writing programs have tried to mirror the diversity of undergraduate studies by using "writing across the curriculum" or "writing in the disciplines." In many cases, these terms simply mean that your first-year writing class will include writing and reading assignments that have been selected from the fields of the sciences, social sciences, and humanities. At some schools, however, "topical writing" seminars are taught in diverse fields of study and combine writing instruction with learning about a specific subject. In such programs, your writing teacher may be a sociologist, a philosopher, a biologist, or a psychologist. At many colleges and universities, students are required to take general composition courses in their first year and must then complete one or more designated writing-intensive courses in particular fields of study before they graduate. At a few schools, students can take linked courses, where one course assigns writing in a particular field of study (such as computer science, nursing, or criminal justice) and a linked writing course helps them learn to write effectively in that field.

In addition, undergraduate programs that lead to careers in the sciences and engineering, law, or business often require (or offer as electives) special courses on written and oral communication in those careers. Beyond their required courses, most schools offer a variety of advanced, elective classes that emphasize particular kinds of writing—for example, academic essays, fiction, poetry, scientific and technical writing, autobiography, or journalism.

What do these diverse forms of instruction have in common? And how do they differ from other courses that require lots of writing? After all, you may be taking courses in literature, history, or laboratory science in which all of your main assignments are essays or reports. And in some of these classes teachers may provide extensive instruction, guidance, and feedback to help you complete the assignments effectively.

While this kind of help can be extremely valuable, *in designated writing or communication classes, uses of language are the main objects of attention and instruction.* Such courses offer you the opportunity to focus not just on the ideas and information you present but also on forms and methods of presentation, from the structures of sentences to the organization of the entire work, along with the process of writing and revision. Such instruction requires amounts of time and attention to language that other types of courses can rarely offer.

Writing Centers and Other Assistance

Because difficulties with writing are normal for writers at all levels of ability and experience, almost every school maintains a writing center where you can get additional help with specific projects or problems. At these writing centers, staff members or peer tutors are available for consultation on writing projects, and many of these centers offer other services, such as courses, workshops on particular skills, libraries of writing resources, Web sites, or online exchanges. College writing centers with more extensive online resources, such as the Online Writing Lab (OWL) at Purdue (http://owl.english.purdue.edu) allow open access to their sites. If writing services at your own school are limited, therefore, you can find extensive information and assistance through the Web. In some cases, writing centers are components of larger programs for developing learning skills, including reading, speaking, study skills, and time management.

In the first year of college, students are sometimes reluctant to use these resources because they view them as "remedial" services that are designed for poor writers. This misconception may be a vestige of high school experience, in which the need for "extra help" usually means that students are falling behind their peers in particular subjects. You should think of writing centers and other services that offer "extra help" not as remedial assistance but as distinctive features of college studies, available and potentially useful to everyone. The most successful college students are often the most likely to use writing centers, peer tutoring services, faculty office hours, or extra review sessions to improve their work. Do not hesitate to use these resources or to consult with your writing teacher when you run into problems with writing assignments in your other courses.

In college as in high school, competitive grading may also appear to support this idea that all learning and performance represent, and measure, individual ability and that good students should be able to do everything on their own. Keep in mind, however, that scholarship is a collaborative endeavor. The great majority of your teachers depend on help from colleagues, mentors, peer reviewers, editors, and others to improve the quality of their research and writing. The best writers and scholars often ask for and receive the most assistance from others. In this sense, writing courses, writing centers, and other services provide forms of collaborative assistance on which all writing and learning can flourish.

GUIDELINES

- Specific uses of language—in *writing, reading, speaking,* and *listening*—determine the kinds of learning that occur in all courses, along with the variations among them. A successful transition to college therefore requires flexible adjustment to these uses of language and their variations.

- Taking notes in class, for example, is a form of *writing* that also involves *listening* to teachers and usually *reading* information they present. For this reason, listening and looking for the structure of a lecture and recording that structure is more effective than "stenography": trying to write down *everything* teachers say.

- Like other approaches to writing and learning, your note-taking strategies should vary from one course to another. In some classes, reflective notes (pp. 23–25) will provide a necessary basis for writing and discussion.

- In their diverse forms (pp. 25–27), first-year writing classes are designed to help you make the transition to writing and learning in college. You should view them as points of departure for a lifelong process of learning to communicate effectively, not as remedial instruction or as the end of required English.

- College writing centers and related services also support the ongoing development of writers at all levels of ability and experience. Successful college students use these services freely to improve their work.

3 | Reading
How to Stay on Top of It

Reading involves a fair measure of push and shove. You make your mark on a book and it makes its mark on you. Reading is not simply a matter of hanging back and waiting for a piece, or its author, to tell you what the writing has to say. In fact, one of the difficult things about reading is that the pages before you will begin to speak only when the authors are silent and you begin to speak in their place, sometimes for them, doing their work, continuing their projects, and sometimes for yourself, following your own agenda.

—David Bartholomae and Anthony Petrosky, *Ways of Reading*

Amanda's Question

A couple of years ago, Amanda, a first-year student in my fall term writing class, announced a piece of advice she had picked up from a junior she had met. Amanda said, "She told me the most important thing you need to learn here is what *not* to read!"

I thought about this for a moment and replied, hesitantly, "Well, that's *sort of* true." But Amanda looked more distressed than enlightened. "What's the matter?" I asked.

"She didn't tell me *how* you know what not to read," Amanda replied.

Amanda was in the School of Industrial and Labor Relations, ILR, which students claim means "I Love Reading." Her courses in labor history, economics, human resources, and organizational behavior assigned entire books, articles, and chapters of textbooks each week in preparation for writing assignments and essay exams. Just getting through all of this reading was difficult. Understanding and remembering what she had read, figuring out what was important and unimportant, seemed impossible. And this challenge is not confined to students in ILR, to English majors, or to this university. Science courses assign dense chapters of textbooks and lab manuals, and freshmen in these courses are also completing distribution requirements in the social sciences and humanities, along with writing courses that often require extensive reading. Performance on examinations, problem sets, labs, research projects, and writing assignments depends heavily on knowledge acquired from texts of many kinds. As a consequence, *effective* reading probably represents the most crucial set of skills you can acquire in college, where reading everything thoroughly from beginning to end might be impossible.

This was what troubled Amanda and the other students in my class. They sensed that there was something wrong with their approaches to the great volume of reading in their courses. They had begun to realize that more advanced students often spent less time on assigned readings with better results on exams and papers. Perhaps these juniors and seniors had figured out "what *not* to read," as Amanda's friend suggested, and were able to focus more on the important material. Given a particular assignment, however, the question is not only *Should I read this?* because if the answer is "yes," then you need to ask yourself these other questions:

- *What* am I reading?
- *Why* am I reading it?
- *How* can I read it most efficiently?
- *How* can I remember what I will need to know about it?

These questions acknowledge that reading is not a single kind of activity. Reading can be done in many different styles, with different approaches and strategies, used for specific purposes and for particular kinds of texts. And when I refer to "texts," I mean written documents of all kinds—not only textbooks but other books, essays, articles, or reports. Whether you are reading for pleasure, for general understanding, to prepare for an exam, to write a paper on the subject, or to find specific information, your manner of reading will be customized with different kinds of attention and different kinds of cognition and memory.

Texts are also structured in ways that facilitate certain kinds of reading. Some are meant to be read from beginning to end; others, including most textbooks, present information schematically, with many potential points of entry and direction. If you fall into the task of reading without pausing to consider *what*, *why*, and *how* you are going to read, you might be wasting almost all the time you spend reading.

Becoming a Predatory Reader

In my writing classes I often call this strategic approach *predatory reading* or *reading from the top of the food chain*. Will you, the reader, consume what you need to get out of the text, or will the text consume you?

A colleague once objected to this language because it sounded too aggressive, even violent. She wanted her students to feel that reading was a peaceful, pleasurable activity that transports us to other times and places, other ways of viewing the world. My colleague was describing a wonderful kind of reading experience that I hope all of you have had and will continue to have: letting yourselves become absorbed in good books, drawn into the lives of characters, the chain of events, or the flow of information in the world the author creates.

But this is only one way of reading—for pleasure—and for reasons I'll explain, you will rarely use it in your academic work. To describe alternatives, I use aggressive terms such as *predatory reading* to counteract the passive approaches you might bring with you to college or fall into after you arrive. In most academic work, you can't afford to become consumed by the great volume of reading you must do. Nor can you afford to let your reasons for reading become secondary to the author's reasons for writing. If you do, you won't stay on top of your work; you will just fall into it and become lost. More specifically, falling into assigned reading in a passive, linear fashion will have several unfortunate results:

- You probably won't finish all of the reading assigned.
- You won't remember most of what you read.
- You will have no coherent record to remind you of what you understood *while* you were reading.
- If writing assignments ask questions about the reading that include arguments, interpretations, or your own questions, you won't have immediate responses.

The alternative is to read (as you should also write) always with some conscious *intention*—a deliberate strategy. Staying on top of your reading requires awareness that texts—written documents—are not just linear streams of words but constructed objects. Like other constructed objects, such as a table or a car engine, they are composed of parts that are assembled in a particular order for particular purposes. Understanding them is in large part a matter of knowing how they are constructed. Once you know that, you will also know how to take them apart, rearrange the pieces in ways that are most useful to you, and pull out the parts you want to consume. Predatory reading simply acknowledges that books are, as people say, "food for thought."

For survival, every entering student must learn these strategies for staying on top of assigned reading, and every scholar has already learned them. After visits to faculty offices, undergraduates sometimes express wonder at the vast amounts of knowledge these scholars have consumed. They have seen walls lined floor to ceiling with shelves of books and periodicals. "I can't believe they've read all those books!" students tell me, and I reply, "Well, you're right not to believe it."

The truth, of course, is more complex than a question of having read or not read something. Having a "mastery" of books and articles does not necessarily mean you have read them from cover to cover. Sometimes it means much more, sometimes much less, and almost always something different. More accurately, mastery of published material means knowing (1) what it is, (2) why it was written, (3) how to find information within it, and (4) how to use the material for your own purposes.

Scholars use some books entirely as references—for looking up specific information when they need it. They selectively read certain portions of books or articles and ignore others. In some cases they have only glanced through a work, looking for the main idea or for specific kinds of information. And they have read some of the books, articles, selected passages, or poems on their shelves many times with intense care, underlining sentences and making extensive notes.

Therefore, when teachers assign readings, they do not expect you to read everything from beginning to end. They assume that you will develop a range of reading strategies, as they have done, and that you will choose the methods most appropriate for particular assignments. To understand the functions of these methods, you should first consider how your mind and memory work.

Reading and Memory

While you are reading something for one of your courses, your first goal is to understand what the writer is saying. Although this immediate goal of "reading comprehension" is a necessary part of learning, understanding what you are reading while you are reading it does not, in itself, constitute learning or *working knowledge* of the material of the sort you can use in the future to pass exams, write papers, or participate in discussions. Your understanding does not become useful unless you can remember the material and the way you made sense of it, including critical responses, questions, or points of confusion you need to clarify later.

Not remembering is actually the norm, and forgetting occurs very rapidly unless you take some active measures to retain information. Psychological studies indicate that after reading or listening, people typically forget more than half of what they learned within one hour. Their memory then continues to deteriorate more gradually to about 30 percent after nine hours and to about 20 percent after a week. And these are proportions of what you once knew. If you are tired or distracted and do not "take in" what you read or hear, your retention will be much lower. Without some strategy for controlling memory, what you remember will also be unpredictable. The 20 percent that you recall after a week might not be the information you most need to remember.

This massive loss of memory is normal because we don't want or need to recall most of what occurs to us for more than a few seconds. Some crucial kinds of learning, such as motor skills, are very tenacious. If you learned to ice skate one winter, you did not forget how to do this over the next summer, and the same kind of memory applies to riding a bicycle, typing, or throwing a ball. In general, however, we register a very small proportion of the sensory information available to us, and we retain most of this registered information only momentarily, just long enough to steer ourselves through immediate experience.

While you are reading, therefore, you will normally recall what you previously read just long enough to maintain a sense of connection with the sentences you are currently reading. This brief storage period is called *short-term memory*. Unless you take deliberate measures to shift important information into *long-term memory* (something like hitting the SAVE button on your computer), the bulk of what you read will simply evaporate. Even if the material seemed perfectly clear to you at the time, an hour, day, or week later you won't be able to retrieve most of it, and what you do recall has probably meshed with some prior framework or association you brought to the reading. You might remember an example involving cats simply because you love animals or miss your pet at home, not because this example was central to the text. Otherwise you will be left with very general, long-term *impressions* of reading: a vague recollection that the subject was interesting or uninteresting, that you disagreed with the author but not why, or that it made you sleepy.

Continuous streams of information will not end up in long-term memory unless you actively construct a framework for remembering and retrieving what is important—some kind of *mnemonic* or aid to your memory. In other words, you need to break up the stream and repackage it somehow. On average, for example, people can't store memory of more than seven random numbers, which explains the standard length of telephone numbers, why we can remember them, and why most of us can't remember the numbers on our credit cards. But we can recall longer sequences of numbers if we cluster them into logical units or create some other mnemonic. We "package" the long-distance area code separately and attach it to local numbers, or we locate logical sequences, repetitions, multiples, and sound patterns. For example, the number 321-1428 is easier to remember than an unpatterned string like 738-4192 if you register the fact that 321 is an inverted sequence and that *one times four times two equals eight.* What we initially remember, then, is not the whole but the mnemonic: *the framework for remembering.*

This is why you take notes in lectures. You know you won't remember much of this stream of spoken words unless you make a record of what the teacher said. And because you can't record everything, you need to identify important information and write it down in some kind of logical framework that will later remind you of the whole. You will remember the lecture initially by referring to your notes: the mnemonic you constructed for the purpose of remembering. As my classmate in Western Civilization demonstrated, good lecture notes repackage the material more efficiently than the lecture itself by clustering the information into memorable categories, subcategories, and lists. For the purpose of studying or writing a paper on the topic, reading effective notes can be *more* useful and efficient than listening to the entire lecture again, because these notes have already digested the material in ways you can understand and will therefore reconstitute your own comprehension. For the purpose of taking exams or writing papers, *your* comprehension, not your teacher's, is more essential.

The streams of words you read are equally unmemorable, but students are much less likely to repackage what they read with outlines or notes. The main reason, I suppose, is that a text is objectively *there* when you finish reading it. You can always come back to it, as to a transcript of a lecture, and read it over. But rereading a text is no more efficient than passively listening to a lecture again. You are still left with no record, no mnemonic, to shift your short-term comprehension into lasting memory—into real learning and working knowledge.

Ways of Reading

To accomplish this transfer, for specific purposes, you need a repertoire of reading strategies.

Passive, Linear Reading

You are in a linear mode of reading when you begin with the first word of a text and continue to the last word, letting the linear sequence of words dictate the order in which you encounter information. This way of reading is entirely passive if you don't bring any goals or strategies to the task but simply follow the linear flow of the sentences with your eyes and mind and let the writing just happen.

In this passive mode of reading, what actually happens to you depends on many variables over which you have little control, such as your level of alertness, the qualities of the writing, and your interest in the subject. How much you understand and remember, a week later, will also depend on these variables. If you are tired, if the writing is abstract and tedious, and if the subject doesn't engage your interest, the drone of words might become sedative. You might get to the end of a chapter and have no recollection at all of what you just read. Even if you are alert and interested, your memory of the text a week later might be very sketchy, because passive reading stimulates long-term memory more or less at random, if at all. In this mode, which I call *falling into the text*, readers are vulnerable to the writing and to other factors that surround the act of reading, such as preoccupations, distractions, and patterns of association (or disassociation) with the content.

This is the way you *want* to read a really good novel: simply for pleasure. Just open it to the first page, start reading, and let the flow of language carry you off on a literary journey. If it's a compelling book, you will become absorbed in it, and that's where the pleasure lies. The events and characters might become so real in your imagination that you forget you are reading—forget that they are inventions constructed out of language on the page. The effect is essentially like watching a wonderful movie and forgetting that you are in a theater, watching actors performing a script under direction and on constructed sets, all on film that is projected on a screen.

But this kind of intense absorption, this surrender to the medium, does not necessarily create memory. The most immediately gripping novels, such as thrillers and mysteries, often leave very little lasting recollection beyond a vague memory of fear or suspense. Becoming passively absorbed in a book doesn't leave you in a very good position to take an examination on it a week later or to write a summary or critical review.

This is why passive, linear reading isn't very useful in academic work. Apart from the fact that this manner of reading doesn't reliably engage long-term memory, most of the reading you do in college won't capture and hold your attention like a good novel. If you surrender to it, allow yourself to become absorbed, it may just put you to sleep.

Unfortunately, passive, linear reading is, for most people, the default mode—when they haven't decided to read in a particular way or, aren't even aware that there are options. More than half of the freshmen in my classes initially try to read their textbooks and other assignments in this fashion: starting with the first word of a chapter and continuing to the end, trying to stay alert and receptive, hoping they will remember what they have read. Unless they take steps to deliberately read in a different way, however, they won't remember very much.

Reading with Two Minds

What should you do if the assigned reading *is* a good novel, biography, history, or some other engaging work that you are supposed to read from beginning to end, with interest and pleasure? Some of the analytical reading methods I'll describe in this chapter won't work very well for the kinds of writing in which central themes, conflicts, and meanings develop through continuous stories. When teachers assign this kind of literature, they usually hope you will read it thoroughly and *appreciate* its narrative qualities. Yet they will also expect you to *remember, describe, analyze,* and *evaluate* these features of the text in class discussions and in writing. If you just let yourself "fall into the text" passively and become absorbed in reading, you probably won't have much to say about it a few days later. You may run into the same problem in courses that include films. You will have to let yourself become absorbed in a film to appreciate its qualities, but recalling that you enjoyed a movie or wept at the end won't give you much to say in an assigned paper or a class discussion. Your teacher will also expect you to understand how the director, scriptwriters, and actors *constructed* that experience.

How can you meet both of these expectations: for *appreciation* and for *critical analysis*? Ideally, you would watch the film or read the text at least twice—once straight through for appreciation and then analytically or critically, while taking notes, to determine how it works and what you want to say about it. And if the assigned readings are short stories, essays, or poems, you should have time to read them more than once, with a different strategy each time. If you are supposed to read a long novel in a short time, however, multiple readings may be impossible.

Critics who review films or live performances, such as plays, have to contend with the same challenge. They need to let the performance affect them as it would other members of the audience. At the same time, they must consider how the film or play produced those effects, because they know they will have to describe and evaluate the production in writing. For this purpose, they have learned to attend performances with two minds, one receptive and the other analytical and critical. And in that second, analytical endeavor, they usually take lots of notes during or immediately after the event because they know they can't trust their memories.

With practice, you can cultivate this two-minded way of reading as well: experiencing the qualities of a novel, for example, while considering *how* the novel produced those effects. However real the characters, settings, and events may seem, remember that the author created those experiences of reading out of words and sentences on the page. Assignments will usually ask you to explain how this literary construction project works. As a college sophomore in a literature course, for example, Louisa Bennion introduced her essay on two stories by James Joyce with her own view of their central features and effects, presented imaginatively as a set of instructions:

Start with a character, a very commonplace sort of character, with little to distinguish him but the fact that he is suddenly the subject of a story. Follow him through a series of ordinary, everyday experiences, which may take place in the course of a single evening or may happen over an unspecified amount of time. Make these experiences somehow lead your character into a "sudden intuitive perception of or insight into the reality or essential meaning" of his existence, and you will have created a story about an epiphany. If you are the kind of writer who can do magical and moving things with language, your readers, like that character, will feel that something momentous has occurred, that they too have received some sort of insight or revelation, through the ordinary act of reading a story.

This is the kind of story James Joyce has written in "Araby" and "The Dead." (9)

In preparation for writing this kind of analytical paper, like film critics, you will need to record your reactions and their causes in some detail; otherwise, you won't remember them. Here are some strategies for capturing ideas for writing:

- If you can read the book only once, you should take notes while you read, either on the pages of the book itself or in a separate notebook or electronic document. In the latter case, be sure to record the page numbers or chapters these notes refer to, so you can find the passages easily when you begin to write.

- If you want to avoid disrupting your engagement with the flow of the writing, pause to take notes at intervals, such as the ends of chapters or whenever you take a break from reading. Then you can also quickly skim portions you have read to recall structures, themes, or events.

- Discuss the book with friends or with other students in the class. You probably know from experience that conversations or arguments about a book or a movie stimulate both thought and memory. Discussions lead you to analyze, explain, and perhaps justify your own impressions in ways that help to prepare you for writing.

Highlighting

Those of you who have tried to study textbooks by reading them passively, hoping that you will easily absorb what you need to know, have probably realized that you need to be *doing something* to make important material soak in. This activity on your part is what distinguishes passive reading from *studying*: *examining* something in the effort to understand it. But when you study a text, what exactly should you be doing?

When they reach the end of a textbook chapter and can't remember what they read at the beginning, students typically resort to highlighting the passages that seem important. This use of transparent markers has largely replaced the older practice of underlining, which has the same function. If you buy used textbooks, you might find that someone has already performed this task, sometimes in two or three colors to distinguish categories or levels of importance. I've seen used textbooks that were almost completely highlighted. Apparently *everything* was important.

As a learning tool, highlighting has some values and limitations that you should consider before you fall into the habit. I'll start with the advantages:

- Because you are doing something with and to the text, highlighting keeps you more alert and allows you to read longer without becoming distracted and fatigued.

- Figuring out what you should highlight helps you to understand what you are reading and to determine whether you understand it. If you don't know what is important enough to highlight, you probably don't yet understand the material or why it was assigned.

- Highlighting creates the beginning of an analytical understanding of texts, of the way they are structured. When pulled out of the text, highlighted passages should resemble an outline or summary of the work.

- Perhaps the main advantage of highlighting is the reduction of study time later on, when you need to read through the material again in preparation for an exam or a writing assignment and find you remember almost nothing. If you have left a textbook chapter unmarked, you will have to spend almost as much time reading it again. If you have effectively marked the most important parts, you can sometimes review only those highlighted portions and reduce your study time by more than half.

For some purposes, however, highlighting itself is a waste of time or an insufficient aid to learning. Here are some of the limitations:

- Highlighting (or underlining) alone simply emphasizes the authority of the text: what its author says, believes, or knows. The practice therefore leads you toward memorization and repetition, not toward interpretation, inquiry, or criticism. As a consequence, highlighting works best as a preparation for "objective" examinations of your knowledge or for writing summaries. It is *not* sufficient preparation for raising questions; participating in discussions; or writing arguments, analyses, and interpretations based on readings.

- While it can lead you toward a systematic understanding of the text, highlighting does not effectively *represent* systematic understanding of the material as a structure of information and ideas, even if you use several colors. Highlighting usually emphasizes a linear series of important points, not the connections among them.

- If you need only to grasp and retain the general idea or a few specifics, highlighting while you read is an inefficient, sometimes pointless activity. There are much better strategies, which I'll describe later.

- Highlighting doesn't create long-term memory. When the practice becomes routine, as a way of marking what you need to study later, it can even reduce your memory.

- While thoughtful, effective highlighting can make studying more efficient, inaccurate highlighting can get you into trouble. If you highlight in a linear fashion while you read, you might not recognize important passages the first time through. If you miss them and study only the highlighted portions later, this practice can actually lower your performance on exams.

The most effective highlighting does not simply flag all of the passages you should read again when exams approach. It should also create a framework for understanding and remembering what you have read. That framework is usually built into the text as a logical structure of ideas and information. Highlighting should help to make that structure visible, and observing the ways in which texts are structured can also help you write more effectively. As a consequence, highlighting works best when paired with a nonlinear reading strategy such as *analytical scanning* (see p. 51).

At every level of organization, from the structure of a paragraph to the design of an entire book, there is usually a *main idea* followed by *supporting points*, often leading to *conclusions*. In a book this structure consists of several layers. The entire volume has one main idea or topic. Subtopics of this general theme are also the main topics of individual chapters, which are often subdivided into sections, each with its own central theme. A paragraph, the smallest unit of organization, will also have a topic, supporting points, and sometimes a conclusion.

As a rule (though one with many exceptions), *main ideas appear at beginnings, conclusions at ends, and supporting points in between.* Authors usually present the central theme of a book in the introduction—usually toward the beginning—and present their conclusions at the end. The theme of a chapter also tends to appear at the beginning, as does the topic sentence of a paragraph. Textbooks (and sometimes other books and articles) usually provide summaries at the ends of chapters.

If you are aware of this conventional structure, you can locate main points more easily and recognize the supporting points that follow. For this purpose two colors of highlighter are useful—one to mark the main ideas and the other to indicate supporting points within a section. Double and single underlining can serve the same purpose.

For example, consider this passage from Edward O. Wilson's book *The Diversity of Life*:

Evolution is blinkered still more by the fact that the frequency of genes and chromosomes can be shifted by pure chance. The process, an alternative to natural selection called genetic drift, occurs most rapidly in very small populations. It proceeds faster when the genes are neutral, having little or no effect on survival and reproduction. Genetic drift is a game of chance. Suppose that a population of organisms contained 50 percent A genes and 50 percent B genes at a particular chromosome site, and that in each generation it reproduced itself by passing on A and B genes at random. Imagine that the population comprises only five individuals and hence 10 genes on the chromosome site. Draw out 10 genes to make the next generation. They can all come from one pair of adults or from as many as five pairs of adults. The new population could end up with exactly 5 A and 5 B genes, duplicating the parental population, but there is a high probability that in such a tiny sample the result instead will be 6 A and 4 B, or 3 A and 7 B, or something else again. Thus in very small populations the percentages of alleles can change significantly in one generation by the workings of chance alone. That in a nutshell is genetic drift, about which mathematicians have published volumes of sophisticated and usually incomprehensible calculations.

But let us go on. Population size is critical in genetic drift. If the popu-lation were 500,000 individuals with 500,000 A genes and 500,000 B genes, respectively, the picture would be entirely different. At this large number, and given that even a small percentage of the adults repro-duced—say 1 percent reproduced—the sample of genes drawn would remain very close to 50 percent A and 50 percent B in each generation. In such large populations genetic drift is therefore a relatively minor fac-tor in evolution, meaning that it is weak if opposed by natural selection. The stronger the selection, the more quickly the perturbation caused by drift will be corrected. If drift leads to a high percentage of B genes but A genes are superior in nature to B genes, the selection will tend to return the B genes to a lower frequency. (81)

This is a clear, concise explanation of genetic drift as a factor in evolution, and while you were reading it, you probably felt that you understood what Wilson was saying. But if someone asked you to write a brief explanation of genetic drift two weeks from now, your memory of the passage will have faded considerably. If *The Diversity of Life* were assigned reading in a biology or environmental studies course, your immediate understanding would be of little value unless you take mea-sures to recall this knowledge and study efficiently when you face an exam or writing assignment.

Highlighting can serve this purpose if you imagine what would most efficiently stimulate understanding after short-term memory has faded. If you highlight the main structure of the explanation, this pro-cess will also strengthen your immediate understanding and enhance memory when you look at the passage again.

What should you highlight? As in most explanations and argu-ments, Wilson introduces central topics toward the beginnings of para-graphs, devotes the middle portions to examples, and ends paragraphs with conclusions. Highlighting should underscore this structure, and *highlighted material should read, ideally, as a brief summary of the entire pas-sage.* Here is one way to highlight the structure of Wilson's explanation:

*Evolution is blinkered still more by the fact that the frequency of genes and chromosomes can be shifted by pure chance. The process, **an alter-native to natural selection called genetic drift,** occurs most rapidly in very small populations. It proceeds **faster when the genes are neutral,** having little or no effect on survival and reproduction. **Genetic drift is a*** *game of chance. Suppose that a population of organisms contained 50 percent A genes and 50 percent B genes at a particular chromosome site, and that in each generation it reproduced itself by passing on A and B genes at random. Imagine that the population comprises only five individuals and hence 10 genes on the chromosome site. Draw out 10 genes to make the next generation. They can all come from one pair of adults or from as many as five pairs of adults. The new population could end up with exactly 5 A and 5 B genes, duplicating the parental population, but there is a high probability that in such a tiny sample the result instead will be 6 A and 4 B, or 3 A and 7 B, or something else again.* **Thus in very small populations the percentages of alleles can change significantly in one generation by the workings of chance alone.** *That in a nutshell is genetic drift, about which mathematicians have published volumes of sophisticated and usually incomprehensible calculations.*

But let us go on. **Population size is critical in genetic drift.** *If the population were 500,000 individuals with 500,000 A genes and 500,000 B genes, respectively, the picture would be entirely different. At this large number, and given that even a small percentage of the adults reproduced—say 1 percent reproduced—the sample of genes drawn would remain very close to 50 percent A and 50 percent B in each generation.* **In such large populations genetic drift is therefore a relatively minor factor in evolution, meaning that it is weak if opposed by natural selection.** *The stronger the selection, the more quickly the perturbation caused by drift will be corrected. If drift leads to a high percentage of B genes but A genes are superior in nature to B genes, the selection will tend to return the B genes to a lower frequency. (81)*

Here I've used bold type to highlight the most central points and underlining to indicate supporting points. A quick glance at the examples between would be sufficient to remind you of the details used to illustrate these central statements.

Note that although you can look for important statements *toward* the beginning and end of paragraphs (or sections, or chapters), those statements are not necessarily the first or last sentences. To highlight effectively, you need to read analytically and locate structural features.

Again, highlighting is most effective as an aid to studying the text later if you need only to understand and remember important information. If you want to avoid reading the text again or if you are supposed to read and respond to it critically, other approaches to reading will be more effective.

Notes, Outlines, and Summaries

Students are often surprised that weeks or months later I can sometimes remember papers they wrote for my class, perhaps more vividly than they can. They say, "You must have a really good memory." But I don't. The reason is that I don't only read their papers; I also write extensive comments both in the margins and at the end. In those comments I try to explain what I got out of the paper and what I thought the writer was trying to do, along with evaluations of the work. *I remember their writing as the object of my own active attention and response.*

You will notice the same kind of enhanced recollection if you discuss a book with a friend shortly after you read it, describe it to someone in a letter, or write an essay about it. These active responses will stimulate lasting memory of the book much more effectively than just reading or highlighting. Much later you will remember what *you* said—the way *you* described the book and what *you* liked or disliked about it—more vividly than the aspects you did not describe. Writing and speaking are in themselves *mnemonics*: They help to create long-term memory.

A sense of urgency, a desire to get the reading done, might convince you that pausing to make notes, construct outlines, or write summaries would be a waste of your time, since the author has already written what you need to know. Why rewrite it or write about it at all? Most textbook chapters are already outlined, in a sense. The material is usually broken down into sections, with headings and subheadings, often with numbered lists of points and boldfaced indications of important terms. Textbooks often include chapter summaries that digest the material for you, along with study questions to help you make sure you understand it.

Until you make this structure meaningful in your own terms, however, it will remain the structure of the text and will represent the author's knowledge, not yours. If you can explain the material to someone else, summarize it in your own words, or outline the structure, the knowledge is yours in two ways:

1. This linguistic processing will engage long-term memory.

2. In a summary or outline you will have a record of your own understanding—something you can read quickly later to refresh your memory.

The framework of a good outline will also stimulate recollection of details, examples, or supporting arguments. Even if you can't recall these specifics without reading the material again, the structure of your outline will allow you to scan the text quickly, filling in the pieces you have forgotten. If it is sufficiently clear, a brief outline or diagram can even *eliminate* the need to read the text again. Without rereading, the following outline would recall the substance of Wilson's explanation of genetic drift in the previous excerpts, including the examples:

> Genetic drift
> —alt. to nat. selection
> —rapid in small pop.
> —if not working *against* nat. selection
> —"game of chance"
>   ex: 5 A & 5 B = 6 A & 4 B or 3 A & 7 B
>   500,000 A & 500,000 B = about 50/50%

Like highlighting, however, an outline reaffirms the structure and substance of the text, not your own position in relation to the text. For this reason, notes, either in the margins or in a separate notebook, are especially important if writing assignments or essay exams ask you to respond to readings. If you make notes while you read, you will have a record of your responses to the text: points of agreement or disagreement, alternative interpretations, correspondence or contrast with other readings, or unanswered questions. These notes on your thoughts about the text will put you in a stronger position to develop arguments, interpretations, or comparisons than you would be if you had only read the work passively without paying attention to the way it struck you.

Hard Reading

These active strategies become essential if assigned readings are for some reason very difficult to understand—extremely abstract and complex, technical, archaic, or poorly written. If you can't immediately grasp what the author is saying, your first tendency may be to give up, perhaps with the conclusion that you just aren't smart enough to understand. But there are other more likely reasons why academic writing can be difficult to read, and if you need to understand material that doesn't initially make sense, you have to use your own intelligence to *make sense of it* in terms *you* can remember.

When reading textbooks designed for student readers at particular levels, you may have to look up words you don't understand or study a passage before it seems clear to you. But college teachers often assign scholarly books and articles that were written primarily for readers with extensive knowledge and familiarity with the subject. Understanding this material may require complex and unfamiliar ways of thinking, including basic assumptions the authors do not bother to explain. Here, for example, is the sentence with which the French anthropologist Pierre Bourdieu begins the first chapter, called "The Objective Limits of Objectivism," of his book *Outline of a Theory of Practice* (1977), which is sometimes assigned in social science classes:

> *The practical privilege in which all scientific activity arises never more subtly governs that activity (insofar as science presupposes not only an epistemological break but also a social separation) than when, unrecognized as privilege, it leads to an implicit theory of practice which is the corollary of neglect of the social conditions in which science is possible. (1)*

Although this sentence is extremely complex and circular, the main problem is not that it is poorly written (or poorly translated from the original French). Instead, writing primarily for scholars who are familiar with basic issues in social theory and the philosophy of science, Bourdieu begins his book by throwing us into the middle of ongoing discussions about the problem of "objectivity" suggested in the chapter title. For other readers who aren't already familiar with these issues, just reading the sentence passively (or reading it again and again) won't shed much light on its meaning. The sentences that follow aren't much help either. Highlighting or trying to memorize Bourdieu's language will also be pointless if you don't understand what he means.

To grasp this kind of writing, you must build the context, or frame of reference, in which it does make sense to intended readers. Course lectures, discussions, or other readings will usually provide that context. If you were reading Bourdieu for an anthropology or sociology course, for example, you would know that although he refers to "science" in general, he's concerned primarily with social research and with the social dimensions of all science. From the chapter title and from parts of this sentence, you could figure out that he is addressing the scientific goal of objectivity (perceiving objects of study as they really are), which must result from separation of the observer from the observed. Bourdieu describes this separation as a position of "privilege." For example, the attempt to observe a social group from a privileged position of objectivity will necessarily limit your understanding of what it means to be a member of that group.

If you can build such a frame of reference for understanding the sentence, you can also produce a version that will be easier to remember in the future: *Separation (or "privilege") always governs scientific theory and practice, but it does so especially when scientists fail to recognize this influence.*

Other kinds of assigned reading may be difficult to understand because they *are* badly written. In these cases, too, passive reading, rereading, and highlighting will simply underscore everything that is confusing you. What the author is trying to say, however, is often much simpler than it seems, and you can produce a shorter, clearer version. Your own notes, outlines, and paraphrases can help you escape literature that you hope you never have to read again!

Here is an example of bad writing you would not want to get trapped in: a passage on contractual relations from *The Structure of Social Action* (1949) by the sociologist Talcott Parsons. Try just reading it passively, from beginning to end, and see what happens to you.

> *Spencer's contractual relation is the type case of a social relationship in which only the elements formulated in "utilitarian" theory are involved. Its prototype is the economic exchange relationship where the determinant elements are the demand and supply schedules of the parties concerned. At least implicit in the conception of a system of such relationships is the conception that it is the mutual advantage derived by the parties from the various exchanges which constitutes the principle binding, cohesive force in the system. It is as a direct antithesis to this deeply imbedded conception of a system of "relations of contract" that Durkheim wishes his own "organic solidarity" to be understood.*
>
> *The line which Durkheim's criticism takes is that the Spencerian, or more generally utilitarian, formulation fails to exhaust, even for the case of what are the purely "interested" transactions of the marketplace, the elements which actually are both to be found in the existing system of such transactions, and which, it can be shown, must exist, if the system*

is to function at all. What is omitted is the fact that these transactions are actually entered into in accordance with a body of binding rules which are not part of the ad hoc agreement of the parties. The elements included in the utilitarian conception are, on the contrary, all taken account of in the terms of the agreement. What may, however, be called the "institution" of contract—the rules regulating relations of contract—has not been agreed to by the parties but exists prior to and independently by any such agreement.

The content of the rules is various. (311)

Even the last, and shortest, sentence in the passage—"The content of the rules is various"—can be condensed more effectively to just three words: *The rules vary.* Although Parsons makes everything unnecessarily complicated, he is trying to make a simple yet important distinction between the economic theories of Herbert Spencer and Emile Durkheim. Even this dense, murky version has some obvious structure, and if you examine it analytically, you can see that it consists of a paragraph on the "utilitarian" exchange theory of Spencer and ends with a transition to a following paragraph on the differing views of Durkheim.

Because this is a very abstract explanation of "contractual relations," it might be useful to imagine a more concrete example, such as the sale of a car. The central question is "How do we reach an agreement on the price of this car?" and then "What holds this deal together?" How would Spencer and Durkheim answer these questions?

To construct an understanding I can later remember, I could write a brief summary in my own words:

> *Parsons distinguishes the views of Spencer and Durkheim concerning the bases for "contractual relations": economic transactions and other kinds of agreements. Spencer's "utilitarian" position limits these factors to the individual interests, or "demand and supply schedules," of the parties involved in the agreement. Durkheim argues that all sorts of other "rules," such as laws and customs, govern the terms of contractual relations. Durkheim calls this "organic solidarity."*

If you were about to write a paper or take an essay exam on this material, which would you prefer to have before you—this brief summary paragraph or Parsons's original passage? For a similar purpose, I could create a "mnemonic diagram" of the passage:

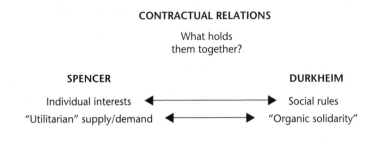

Some Other Ways to Read

When using the methods of reading described in previous sections, you will probably need to go through the text at least once, pausing to highlight material, to take notes, or to construct outlines and diagrams. But you can go through a text and get what you need from it in many ways, ways that are more or less linear or much faster or slower, depending on your reasons for reading.

Reference.   We think of "reference" books as volumes such as dictionaries or encyclopedias, but almost any book can be used primarily as a reference. When you pull such a book off the shelf, you probably turn straight to the index or table of contents. In a volume on the premodern history of China, for example, you might be interested only in the Shang Dynasty or only on the art or religion of this period. *Every book with an index is potentially an encyclopedia on its own subject.*

Supplementary readings on a course syllabus are often intended for use as references, and you will also use books and articles as references when you write research papers, as we will see in Chapter 8. The list of "Works Cited" in a bibliography does not necessarily mean that the writer has read all of this material from beginning to end.

Selective reading.   In some cases only certain portions of a book, or particular articles in a journal, are immediately important. Scholars therefore might have read these sections very closely while ignoring or only glancing at everything else. Scientists and social scientists selectively read many research articles, looking only at the abstract or the introduction, perhaps, to see what the article is about or at the methods, figures, specific results, or conclusions, depending on their interests. We also read selectively while looking through magazines, reading only the first paragraph or the sidebars or just looking at the pictures and captions.

Analytical scanning.   You might imagine that analytical scanning is the same as "skimming," but in some respects it is the opposite. Skimming is cruising quickly over the surface to get a general sense for the content. The effect resembles the view you get through the window of an airplane or high-speed train: a stream of blurred, general impressions. Analytical scanning is more like examining a topographical map or aerial photograph of a whole area: studying the structure of the landscape and noting high points or centers of importance. Not bound to any linear path, your vision can move in any direction, focus closely, or widen to encompass the whole.

When scanning a book, you might begin by examining the table of contents to see how the work is organized and, in a very general way, what it contains. Then, to figure out what the author is trying to do—the *purpose* of the book—you might scan the introduction, focusing especially on the beginning and end, where authors are most likely to state their intentions. Then you might skip to the last chapter, where you are likely to find conclusions or summaries of the entire work. With this knowledge of what the author was setting out to do and then claimed to have done, you can turn back to the beginnings of particular chapters to determine how this goal was accomplished. In these chapters, as in the entire volume, you will usually find the most central points at the beginning and end. These methods are especially useful for studying textbook chapters, which are often designed for nonlinear, analytical reading. Clever students have told me that when textbook chapters list study questions at the end, they read these first as indications of what is most important and then look for answers.

The best way to teach yourself effective scanning is to give yourself far too little time to figure out what a book or chapter says—a time so brief that linear, continuous reading is impossible.

For a ten-page article, for example, give yourself only ten minutes to figure out what the author is saying and to write a one-paragraph summary. For a book, give yourself only thirty minutes to grasp its main ideas and organization and write a one-page summary.

If you become adept at analytical scanning, you can "read" an entire book in twenty or thirty minutes. If you take notes in the process, you will end up with a more useful understanding of its content than you would have if you had spent several hours reading it from cover to cover in a passive, linear fashion.

Close reading. While selective reading and analytical scanning are much faster than reading through a text from beginning to end, word by word, some assignments will require much more time and attention. Extremely difficult texts, extremely important ones, an essay you will discuss in class, or a poem you must interpret in a writing assignment might require several readings and careful analysis.

As a consequence, the length of a reading assignment bears little relation to the time you might spend on it. Although it might be possible to pick up the central themes of an entire book in thirty minutes, you might need to spend one hour reading two pages of an important essay or one short poem. Students often tell me fatalistically that they *have* to spend a certain amount of time reading a certain number of pages, as though this pace were unalterable. From my perspective, this simply means they are stuck in a certain way of reading. In some respects, close reading and analytical scanning are related strategies, not opposites. In both cases you are analyzing the structure of the text, moving back and forth through it, not bound to follow its linear order.

> Try using analytical scanning and close reading on the same text. Give yourself only fifteen minutes to scan a whole chapter of one of your textbooks to figure out the overall structure and content. Then spend fifteen minutes closely studying a specific section of less than one page, examining the way this information is presented and outlining or summarizing the content.

Overcoming Resistance to Strategic Reading

You may ask, if the reading strategies I've described are so effective, why do most students still read their textbooks from beginning to end, a highlighter poised over the page, just waiting for the chance to mark something worth remembering?

As I noted previously, a passive, linear approach to reading is the default mode—the easiest way of reading to fall into *without thinking*. And that, of course, is the problem. If you aren't actively thinking about *what* you are reading, *why* you are reading it, and *how* you are reading it, you aren't going to get much lasting value out of the time you spend.

But students cling to reading methods that don't actually work very well in undergraduate studies for other reasons, as well. Students have told me that if they don't read every word in the order in which it appears, they are afraid they will "miss" something. What if something really important lies in one of those parts you skipped over? It seems illogical that you could learn more by reading less or that you could understand something better by spending less time reading it.

The flaw in this reasoning lies in the assumption that you will learn and remember written material simply because your eyes happened to pass over it, following the linear trail of words from beginning to end, or because you covered it with transparent marker. Having read something in this way offers no reliable assurance that you have learned and will remember what you read. In your effort not to miss anything, you might, in the long run, miss almost everything. By the next day you might be left with nothing but a warm sense of virtue for having completed your homework.

> You can test the arguments I've made by reading two different chapters of the same textbook in two different ways and then finding out how much you remember later. Scan one chapter analytically, and outline its content in a few minutes, deliberately searching for important points and structural elements. Spend at least twice as much time reading another chapter from beginning to end, trying simply to absorb the material without taking notes.
>
> Wait at least one day and then try to summarize both chapters from memory, each in a paragraph or two, without looking at the chapters or at the notes you kept on the first. Which one do you remember better?

I've also known people who have a kind of aesthetic objection to reading something "out of order" or selectively—an attitude akin to the moral outrage some people feel toward readers who skip to the end of a novel to find out what happens. From this perspective, the linearity of a book or essay represents its integrity, and reading in a linear fashion demonstrates respect for that integrity. Analytical or selective reading, out of order, therefore violates the integrity of the text, much as dissecting a frog does violence to the living creature.

While analytical reading bears some resemblance to dissection, texts are not like living creatures. You can read them in any order you like, dismantle them, examine their structural elements, take what you want from them in notes, and still be left with an undamaged whole. Then you can return to them, if you like, and read them over in a different way. The same can't be said for highlighting, which really does alter (and even damage) the text. By contrast, the Grand Masters of Strategic Reading would be so skillful and efficient that they could buy all of their textbooks for the term, extract everything they needed from them before the bookstore's full refund deadline expired, and return them unmarked and like new.

GUIDELINES

- Successful students and scholars know that reading is a variety of activities, used for specific purposes. To find the best reading strategy, you should ask yourself *what* you are reading, *why* you are reading it, and *how* you can read it most effectively for that purpose (p. 31).

- For most kinds of academic work, therefore, I encourage you to become "predatory readers": those who choose the best strategy for getting what they need out of a text (pp. 32–33).

- Remember that the goal of most academic reading is to create long-term memory and working knowledge of the material—a goal that passive reading will not fulfill.

- When you begin to read, pause to make sure that the way you are reading corresponds with its functions and your purposes for learning, studying, or writing. The following chart correlates diverse ways of reading with some of their most common functions:

Passive, Linear Reading (p. 36)	For appreciation and general comprehension
Reading with Two Minds (p. 37)	For combining appreciation with critical analysis
Highlighting (p. 39)	For focusing attention, making structural features and important information visible, and facilitating studying in the future
Notes, Outlines, and Summaries (p. 45)	For capturing your own analysis and understanding, including critical perspectives
Hard Reading (p. 46)	For developing your own understanding of writing that doesn't make itself clear to you.
Reference (p. 50)	For locating specific information within texts
Selective Reading (p. 50)	For identifying and grasping the most important texts or portions of them
Analytical Scanning (p. 51)	For understanding the overall structure and purpose of a text quickly, sometimes as a basis for further study
Close Reading (p. 52)	For deep understanding and detailed analysis and criticism

- If you feel that you must read everything from beginning to end, consider your reasons for believing this is necessary. There is no inherent virtue in linear, continuous reading, whereas diversified, strategic reading methods are essential for successful college work.

4 | How Good Writing Gets Written

When you write, you lay out a line of words. The line of words is a miner's pick, a wood-carver's gouge, a surgeon's probe. You wield it, and it digs a path you follow. Soon you find yourself deep in new territory. Is it a dead end, or have you located the real subject? You will know tomorrow, or this time next year.

—Annie Dillard, *The Writing Life*

Patterns of Discontent

College teachers are usually more dissatisfied with student writing than their own students realize. Most college students, in turn, are capable of producing better writing—and writing closer to their teachers' expectations—than they do. In this chapter on writing methods, I'll explain some of the reasons for this distance between what teachers hope to read and what students write. And I'll explain what you can do to reduce this distance, to your own advantage.

Students reasonably assume that grades and comments on their work accurately represent a teacher's evaluations of their writing and of the thinking that writing conveys. If they get a decent grade on a paper and some positive comments, they conclude that the teacher thought their work was at least adequate. And if they are generally satisfied with these grades, students will see little reason to change their writing methods and standards. This complacent attitude can be very frustrating to writing teachers who, from a broader perspective, know why and how student writing will need to improve, especially in advanced studies and careers. In fact, grades and comments tend to *conceal* what teachers actually think about student writing, along with some of its most common weaknesses. How can grades conceal the evaluations they are supposed to represent?

In particular classes, teachers usually adjust their standards for evaluation and grading to the range of writing quality in the papers they read. They sometimes find even the best writing in the class disappointing, and according to their real standards for good writing, teachers may consider average papers to be poorly written. Yet, they will probably give some of the best papers an A. Due to levels of grade inflation at most schools and expectations lowered by past experience, those weak, average papers will usually receive grades of B or B+, with corresponding mixtures of praise and criticism. Individual teachers may use lower grades at the beginning of the term to emphasize common problems and raise general standards for writing in the class. But those who continue to maintain absolute standards for good writing in their grading criteria risk seeming harsh and unfair, with damaging effects on their popularity. Grading practices therefore maintain an illusion among college students that teachers are more or less satisfied with the overall quality of student writing in their classes.

When college teachers talk with one another about student writing, however, their assessments are usually less generous. And although their specific assignments and expectations vary considerably, their descriptions of common weaknesses in student writing are fairly consistent:

- Many student papers "don't have a clear thesis" or they "don't pose and answer a real question."

- The writers haven't sufficiently thought through the topic or issue, and they haven't developed "interesting, original ideas."

- The papers are disorganized; they seem to be "patched together," without sufficient logical development, transitions, and supporting evidence.

- Student writers use and document sources carelessly, without clearly distinguishing their own views and voices from those of others.

- Students "don't revise and proofread their papers," as evidenced by poor word choices and phrasing, grammatical errors, and typos.

In general, teachers view the typical student paper to be comparable to a rough draft that needs further thought, development, revision, and editing.

As generalizations, these critical assessments don't apply to all student writing, nor do they explain *why* such problems are so common. One possible explanation is that college teachers hold unreasonably high standards—beyond the skills and capabilities of most undergraduates. And there is some truth to this. For reasons I explained in Chapter 1, college teachers may assume that you already know how to produce types of writing you have never done before. Learning how to write in new ways, in different fields of study, takes practice, and a lot of the weak writing that teachers complain about results from the unavoidable process of trial and error in learning any new skill. From this perspective, normative grading simply forces teachers to adjust their expectations to the real difficulty of their assignments, in the same way that grading "on the curve" adjusts for the actual difficulty of an exam for the students who took it.

But other, less arbitrary reasons exist for the specific kinds of dissatisfaction with student writing that teachers often express: **Student papers often resemble first drafts of the kind of writing teachers hope to receive because these papers *are* first drafts—unrevised and poorly edited.**

Although undergraduates produce many types of writing for diverse courses, they complete these tasks with surprisingly consistent methods through which they try to avoid extensive revision. These typical methods that students use for completing assignments account for most of the perceived weaknesses in the preceding list: **unclear theses and arguments, insufficient thought about the topic, poor organization and logical development, and careless proofreading.** Problems with documentation and references to sources more often result from a lack of knowledge and experience in ways I discuss in Chapter 7.

Students often tell me that these typical writing methods represent their only realistic options, because busy schedules demand that they develop the most efficient strategies for getting their work finished on time. They argue that further thoughts, extensive revisions, and meticulous proofreading all require time they don't have. But these arguments are only partly valid. Although time constraints do limit the strategies you can reasonably use for completing particular assignments, the writing process still offers many options that produce better writing—the kind that teachers hope to read. The most successful student writers experiment with these alternative strategies and develop more effective writing methods that remain efficient.

To make these alternatives clear, we need to consider how writing actually gets written and how different kinds of writers, including students and scholars, move through this process.

Process and Product

If a friend called while you were working on a writing assignment and asked what you were doing, you would probably just say, "I'm writing a paper," as though writing were a single activity. In fact, at particular moments in the process of working on that paper you might be engaged in very different activities:

- Making notes or outlines
- Reading source material
- Pausing to think about what you were going to write
- Composing new sentences
- Reading over sentences you previously wrote
- Making changes to these sentences or to larger passages
- Checking your work for errors and other problems

These and other activities constitute the process of writing. And in writing, as in other kinds of production, the process directly affects the quality of the product. If we prepare a meal hastily, assembling poor ingredients without much thought or attention, we aren't likely to end up with a tasty dish. The best chefs, like the best writers, refine their methods and think carefully about what they are doing, with close attention to detail.

Individual writers use a great variety of methods, depending on the types of writing they are doing, the time available, and their own preferences. For example, writers may prefer to compose and revise drafts on paper before typing them on a keyboard. Others type directly on a computer, making changes as they compose. Some writers make elaborate plans and outlines before they begin to write a draft; others plunge straight into the task and organize their work as they produce it.

Although individuals move through the writing process in different ways, the scholars who have studied this process found they could sort specific writing activities into categories of thought and behavior.

Here is my own version of these categories, drawn from studies that give them a variety of names:

Prewriting or Planning

At certain times, writers are not actually producing sentences and passages of text but are *preparing* to do so: gathering information and ideas from readings, thinking about the task, making notes or outlines. Even walking or driving, eating lunch, or talking with someone about the project can be considered *prewriting* activities if they stimulate our intention to write.

Composing

At other times, writers are composing new sentences and passages, either on paper or the computer, with the idea that these sentences might, at least, appear in the finished product.

Revising or Rewriting

Revision literally means "to see again," from a somewhat different perspective, and *rewriting* means changing what you have previously written, according to this new way of envisioning the task. Some writers revise entire drafts of complete chapters or essays. Others interrupt the composing phase to revise smaller sections, such as paragraphs, before they move on.

Editing or Proofreading

The boundary between revision and editing is not clearly defined, and in the publishing industry, *editing* can refer to all changes in a manuscript, including broad revisions. For the writing process, however, editing means highly focused attention to specific words or phrases or to the structure of a sentence. This local attention (which includes proofreading for errors and typos or running a document through a spelling checker) differs from revising, which is reconsidering the organization of an entire passage or draft.

Release

"Performance, in which the whole fate and terror rests, is another matter," James Agee said in his introduction to *Let Us Now Praise Famous*

Men, after he had described how he *hoped* his book would affect readers. He knew that while he was writing, this outcome was still unpredictable, somewhat beyond his control. So I include this last phase of the writing process to mark that turning point: when we drop a letter into the mail slot, click the SEND button on an e-mail message, hand in a paper to the teacher, or send a manuscript off to a publisher.

Some accounts of the writing process describe these kinds of activity as "stages," and you can easily imagine how they could be used to formulate a linear prescription for writing—a set of instructions, like a recipe:

1. Figure out what you want to say, and make an outline.
2. Compose a draft according to your outline.
3. Revise your draft.
4. Edit the revised version.
5. Turn in the finished product.

There is a certain amount of sequential logic to the phases of the writing process, especially in retrospect. You can't turn in a paper until it has been written; you can't revise or edit passages until they have been composed; and prewriting, as the term suggests, obviously comes before writing. In high school, you may have been taught to write papers in a comparable series of steps.

In practice, however, writers rarely work in this strictly linear fashion, even when they have been taught to do so. Instead, movement through the writing process is always somewhat "loopy" or *recursive*, even when we are trying to produce something in a single draft. If you pay close attention to what you are doing, you will probably find that you do not produce sentences continuously for more than a minute or two without pausing to read over what you have previously written—to remind yourself of what you have said, to restore a sense of voice and direction, and to gather your thoughts for moving ahead. When you read back over previous sections you might also pause to edit or even to revise what you have written. Phases of *planning*, *revising*, and *editing* are therefore interwoven with *composing* a draft. In a survey of research titled "Understanding Composing," Sondra Perl described these interwoven activities in terms of motion and direction from observing writers at work:

> Throughout the process of writing, writers return to substrands of the overall process, or subroutines (short successions of steps that yield

results on which the writer draws in taking the next set of steps); writers use these to keep the process moving forward. In other words, recursiveness in writing implies that there is a forward-moving action that exists by virtue of a backward-moving action. (364)

As you shift among these "substrands" of the process, progress occurs not in a straight line but in overlapping spirals. Because you are always free to move back and forth among these types of writing activities, at every moment you have a great variety of choices. The specific choices you make will largely determine the quality of the work you eventually produce, along with the time you spend producing it.

The speed with which writers compose a draft therefore depends not only on the number of drafts and revisions they produce but on the amount of time they spend thinking about what they are going to say or reading over, revising, and editing what they have written so far. Those who are trying to make the first draft the last often compose very slowly. In their effort to avoid second or third drafts, they tend to interrupt the flow of their thoughts frequently to look backward and forward, revising, editing, and planning as they compose. In an interview, the anthropologist Clifford Geertz admitted that even though he considered it "a very bad way to do things," he wrote whole articles and books in a single draft:

> *I have an outline, especially if it's a book, but I hardly pay attention to it. I just build it up in a sort of craft-like way of going through it carefully, and when it's done it's done. The process is very slow. . . . I usually write about a paragraph a day, but at least it's essentially finished when it's done. (248)*

As I'll soon explain, college students generally believe that completing a writing assignment in one draft is the fastest, most efficient way to get the writing assignment done. For reasons that Geertz illustrates, this is not necessarily true. Because composing itself is almost always a "loopy" process and not a continuous, linear one, writing a three-page paper in one draft might take an hour, six hours, or several days, depending on the amount of time the writer spends pausing to think, reading over what he or she has written, or reconstructing sentences. For the same reasons, producing three drafts of a paper might be faster than writing one.

The final products of writing, such as finished papers or published books, do not clearly reveal the methods writers used to produce them. If Clifford Geertz did not tell us how he writes, we would not be able to determine just from reading one of his articles or books whether he produced it in one slowly, carefully assembled draft or through multiple drafts with extensive revisions.

In fact, the best writing most effectively *conceals* the history of its production. When you read a beautifully written story or article, the words and sentences flow smoothly, logically, from beginning to end. If you read this work aloud, it will sound like fluent speech. Because you have no way of knowing how it was actually written, the linear flow and natural pace of the writing will invite you to imagine that it was written in the way it reads: that the author knew before she started exactly what she wanted to say, began to write with the first word you see, and continued writing to the last word on the last page. You might imagine that really good writers, like good speakers, can do this gracefully and effortlessly, with no need to pause or revise. The linearity of the product and its association with speech leads people to believe that good writing results from natural eloquence, talent, or inspiration. These factors can also lead us to *attempt* to write in the way we read and speak—from the first word to the last, in a continuous sequence.

But these ideas about the process, derived from the product, are for the most part fictions. Occasionally, when we are extremely lucky, we can produce good writing easily and quickly, in a single draft. But more often than not, the best writing results from extensive revision, much as good performances in music, theater, or dance result from extensive practice and rehearsal. Like other performing arts, writing gives us the opportunity to compose, rehearse, and revise before the real performance—the moment when the audience actually reads what we have written.

Because the product conceals the process, students know very little about the methods their teachers and other scholars use to meet standards for publication. While these standards do not directly determine a teacher's criteria for grading student papers, they do influence the assessments of weaknesses in student work that were listed at the beginning of the chapter.

One college senior realized what this process of writing for publication entails when he coauthored a research article for a biology journal with one of his professors:

This paper isn't revolutionary, or even very important. However, it is around twenty pages of material (including several figures and mathematical models) that was examined, criticized, corrected, submitted, returned, resubmitted, returned, etc., and finally published. What it taught me was that to know what you want to say, to know you've got to be concise, to understand you have to have a special format, and to work hard on putting a paper together never means you are going to produce a perfect paper. No one ever has, no one will. But all I wanted was to get our paper accepted, and that was almost impossible, too. The only way I think people will realize the effort that has to be put into a paper to raise it to the standards of a good journal and hard, cold (maybe not, but still undeniably hard) reviewers is for them to publish.

The long, frustrating process this student described is familiar to scholars in every field. One scientist told me that he had thirty-six drafts of his most recent research article on his computer. Scholars usually show drafts of their work to colleagues and make extensive revisions before they submit articles or book manuscripts for publication. Editors then send these submissions out for "peer review" to other experts in the field. Even if that version is accepted, reviewers and editors usually recommend substantial changes as conditions for publication. And many articles, like the one this student described, are initially rejected and must be revised and resubmitted to different journals before they are accepted. In many cases, the published forms have been revised so thoroughly—even in their central arguments, research claims, and titles—that they bear little resemblance to the original drafts. Due to the complexity of this process, the published essays and articles assigned as readings in your classes usually require months of intermittent work to get into print. Academic books often take years.

Individual scholars get through this process with a great variety of methods and work habits. Revision, for example, may represent a separate stage of rewriting a complete draft, or it may be an ongoing task of making changes, rearranging passages, and adding and deleting while the writer composes. Some scholars complete writing projects on their own, but others (especially in the sciences) collaborate with coauthors throughout the project.

Although their individual writing strategies differ considerably, **all of these scholars know from experience that first thoughts and first**

drafts will rarely turn out to be the best or the last. As one chemist told me, "A first draft confronts you with the nature of your own confusion on the subject. Revision gives you a chance to recover from that confusion." To take advantage of that opportunity, serious writers of all kinds must avoid becoming wedded to the first way they present the original ideas that occur to them. In an early study of "Revision Strategies of Student Writers and Experienced Adult Writers," published in 1980, Nancy Sommers included this professional author's view that revision must remain an open possibility:

> *My cardinal rule in revising is never to fall in love with what I have written in a first or second draft. An idea, sentence, or even a phrase that looks catchy, I don't trust. Part of this idea is to wait a while. I am much more in love with something after I have written it than I am a day or two later. It is much easier to change anything with time.*

The Choices Student Writers Make

In the same study of revision strategies, Nancy Sommers found that college freshmen planned to make the first drafts of their papers the last, and they did not tend to use the terms *revision* or *rewriting* to describe changes they made. Instead, they mentioned minor corrections and deletions they made while "reviewing" their work. In terms of the writing process, once they had planned and composed a paper in one draft, they bypassed revision and simply edited—or proofread—work that they considered finished. One of these students described both the intention and the practice:

> *I don't use the word "rewriting" because I only write one draft and the changes that I make are made on top of the draft. The changes that I make are usually just marking out words and putting different ones in.*

Sommers concluded from this research that college freshmen reduced revision to editing as an "afterthought" to composing a paper, because they confused writing with the linearity of speech. Because the effort to make the first draft the last also forced them to accept first thoughts as the last thoughts, they imagined that good writing resulted primarily from "inspiration," not from rethinking and revising:

I throw things out and say they are not good. I like to write like Fitzger-
ald did by inspiration, and if I feel inspired then I don't need to slash and
throw much out.

This student's reference to Fitzgerald is appropriate in an ironic way. When he was an undergraduate at Princeton, and then in the army, F. Scott Fitzgerald did try to write as this student imagines he did: in single "inspired" drafts. In this fashion he produced his first novel—appropriately titled *The Romantic Egoist*—in only three months, but publishers rejected it because, as biographer Robert Sklar explains, "Fitzgerald lacked the time and the patience to do more than a patch-up job." By the end of Fitzgerald's career, his approach to writing had completely changed. *Tender Is the Night* (the new title) went through roughly seventeen drafts over a period of ten years.

For decades, college writing teachers have tried to persuade students that they should include revision in the process of completing papers. Because typewriters made revision difficult, it was hoped that the flexibility of word processors would encourage students to use the writing process more flexibly as well, especially that they would rethink and revise work in progress. But this revolution in student writing methods did not occur. As a rule, students simply used word processors as sophisticated typewriters: ones on which they could compose papers directly without worrying about minor mistakes.

In other words, both high school and college students tend to use computers as *composing and editing machines*, not as *revising machines*. Although word processors make it easy to move, add, or delete large sections of text; store multiple drafts; or splice sections of one draft into another—options that professional writers routinely use—student writers do not tend to use these features. One reason is that the computer screen conceals most of the document, and to see all the text, one must print out a hard copy. However, it is very easy to make minor changes on the portion of the text that is visible. Automatic checks for spelling, grammar, and style also focus attention on local, visible portions of the document. A word processor cannot point out to you that your paper is a "patch-up job," like Fitzgerald's first novel, or that your argument doesn't make sense.

In spite of great technological changes, therefore, my own investigations of student writing methods correspond closely with those that Nancy Sommers reported more than twenty-five years ago. When they are writing papers or reports *outside* a writing class (where teachers often assign revision), the great majority of college students try to make the first draft the last and avoid substantial revision as much as possible. The linear process my students typically describe is

1. Figure out what you want to say (with or without an outline).
2. Write the paper.
3. Fix it up.
4. Turn it in.

Although there are many variations within this general routine, the majority of students use some version of this sequence even for long papers. This junior, for example, described the way she wrote a thirteen-page analysis of three films:

> *Right from the beginning I knew that my first draft was going to be my last. The only revisions that I made to the first draft of my paper were typos, and* occasionally *I would fix awkward sentences. There were absolutely no changes in the ideas, theme, and organization of the paper because they were already determined before I started writing. Part of the reason I did this was time constraints, but most of the time I just didn't feel like it: the sense of completion was so great that I just couldn't bring myself to go back and correct the paper.*

This "sense of completion"—the overwhelming desire to be finished—is an extremely common theme among student accounts of their writing practices. Some argue, as this junior initially did, that because they knew exactly what they wanted to say, the structure and content of the paper were "already determined" and did not need to be changed. In their desire to finish the task, they convince themselves that their first ideas are also the best or that altering the design of a first draft would ruin it beyond repair. In different parts of an interview quoted below, we can catch this freshman in the act of rationalizing a one-draft approach that is actually driven by procrastination and his desire to "get it over with as soon as possible." Asked how he writes the first draft, this student explained:

> *As a procrastinator I usually put it off 'til the night before; I don't know. I hold it off and I usually spend. . . . I go into the morning. I go into the night writing papers. You know, as you're writing, you know, when it's*

late and you're really tired, your paper starts to get worse and worse, in terms of content. You just want to get it over with. You type in junk, I guess. That's how you think.

Later in the interview, when he was asked whether he makes real changes to the first draft, his viewpoint shifted:

Well, what I have down is basically what I wanted to put in. It's exactly like building a wall—you can't take anything out once you've put it in. I think that each sentence is something I really wanted to express, and just to take it out is like, like breaking the wall down.

Along the same lines, a senior confessed, "When I get an idea on how to approach the subject matter, it is hard for me to let go." The phrases and sentences she has written get "sticky," she said, and make it difficult for her to "restructure" what she has already said. When asked if they ever revised papers, a number of students said that revision was something they did for writing teachers when they were told to turn in rough drafts and then revise.

Cost/Benefit Analysis

I know from experience that if, like the majority of my students, you believe it's perfectly acceptable to try to make the first draft of your writing the last, I can't convince you that you should change your methods without explaining how and why you should do so, or why other students do not. I know that your friends and classmates probably have more influence on your learning strategies than your teachers do, primarily because you study, write papers, and do other assignments with them, not with your teachers.

But students often don't explain *why* they are using one approach or another, and blindly following the crowd can lead to difficulty. The weaknesses in thought, organization, and fluency that teachers commonly observe in student writing characterize *all* rough drafts (including mine) and call for revision and careful editing. Why would the majority of student writers adopt methods that routinely dissatisfy the readers who evaluate their work? If further thought and revision can significantly improve your writing and your grades on written work, why would you choose to ignore this potential advantage?

When I ask my students to answer these questions, they almost invariably mention time constraints and competing priorities as the main reasons for their writing methods. Unlike their teachers, college students rarely have the luxury of developing an essay over a period of weeks or months. Short papers and reports, of three to six pages, are usually due a week or two after they are assigned, and with the exception of writing courses, college teachers rarely make rough drafts and revisions a part of the assignment schedule. Taking four or five courses means students often have more than one writing assignment in a single week. Given these hectic schedules, if they are managing their time well, they need to estimate in advance how many hours they can afford to spend completing a paper and then schedule that time. Procrastinators and others who are *not* managing their time well usually need to complete work in the few hours that remain before a paper is due. For these students, writing methods are no longer a matter of choice. They have to "crank out" a paper in one draft as quickly as possible.

The most obvious benefit of trying to make your first draft the last, therefore, is a Euclidean sense of efficiency. If Point A is the beginning of the writing process and Point B is the finished paper at the end, the most efficient way to get from Point A to Point B is in a series of stages: *prewriting, composing, revising, editing,* and *releasing.* It seems reasonable that eliminating any of these stages will make the process shorter and therefore more efficient. If you can make the first draft the last, you can eliminate the *revision* stage. If you either know exactly what you want to say or can invent an argument as you write, you can streamline *prewriting* as well. And if you can write carefully enough in this draft, you can even dispense with *editing.* Then, in theory, the process would be reduced to its most "efficient" form, closest to the linearity of speech: *Just write the paper and turn it in!*

According to this linear logic, any further thoughts, reorganization, rewriting, and other procedural "loops" always make the writing process messier, slower, and less efficient. And I know from experience how compelling this logic can be when you are juggling several responsibilities in a busy semester. In one advanced writing class I taught, I completed some of the writing I assigned to my students and exchanged drafts of my work with other writers in peer review groups. On the first of these assignments, I convinced myself that I could produce a decent argument in a couple of hours, without revision. I was very busy that week, and after all, I told myself, I was the most capable, experienced writer in my class. In the process of writing, I was vaguely aware that I was really making *two* arguments that didn't quite fit together, but I didn't think my readers would even notice—especially if I used clever transitions that obscured the faulty logic. So I felt just as annoyed and dismayed as my own students do when my readers told me I really needed to rewrite the paper. At the end of her thoughtful, written comments on my work, one student concluded:

> *I understand the shaky relationship you are drawing between these two subjects, and I mean it in the nicest possible way to say that as a reader, you don't carry me through—I feel pushed around and left wandering. I think this paper would be improved if you ruthlessly cut one subject or another and concentrated more fully on a microscopic level. Good luck.*

These comments were remarkably similar to the ones I commonly write on papers my students have patched together in one draft and superficially polished to disguise the fact that the arguments don't quite hold together. And my paper contained these common weaknesses because I was using the methods most of my students use, in the same circumstances, and for essentially the same reasons. In believing I could trick my readers, I had actually tricked myself into thinking I didn't really *have* to reconsider and rewrite.

Under certain circumstances, all of us complete writing in one draft, editing as we compose, with no substantial revision. This approach to writing works best under three conditions:

1. You know what you want to say, with a clear sense of form and direction.
2. The task is simple.
3. The stakes and standards for the product are low.

But these conditions do not characterize most formal, graded writing assignments in college. If you do not know what you want to say, if the assignment is complex, or if the stakes and standards for the finished product are high, a one-draft approach can be both unsuccessful and inefficient. My own effort to assemble a complex argument in one quick draft, without knowing exactly what I wanted to say, left my readers confused and simply postponed the unavoidable task of revision. This method has other costs you should consider as well:

- The linear, Euclidean principle of efficiency can only give you the shortest route between Point A and Point B if you know where these points lie—where your paper will begin, where it will end, and what you will say in between. Otherwise, writing will be an exploratory process of figuring out what you want to say and how you can best present these thoughts. The most efficient way to figure out what you want to say is a quick, exploratory draft you can then reconsider and revise.

- Exploratory drafts also work best if the assignment calls for a long, complex paper. If you try to plan the paper in advance to avoid revision, you will be stuck with your first thoughts, which probably won't be the most interesting or coherent. If you start from some arbitrary Point A without knowing where the paper will go, you are likely to get lost or change direction.

- If your standards or those of your readers are high, trying to avoid revision simply slows the process of composing to a crawl—or even to a halt. For Clifford Geertz, that effort reduces productivity to one paragraph per day. Other writers with high standards feel that to establish control they must have the work planned in great detail before they start to compose. To avoid revision, therefore, they spend enormous amounts of time in the prewriting phase. I've known several students who experienced writing blocks because they couldn't meet their standards for complex papers in one draft. Without revision, writing seemed impossible.

- The idea that you are producing the finished product, the final performance, will make you more vulnerable to a kind of stage fright. This anxiety produces a writing style I call "gripped": extremely hesitant, tense, cautious, and overly formal. In his book *Writing without Teachers*, Peter Elbow explained this unfortunate effect on style:

The problem is that editing goes on at the same time as producing. The editor is, as it were, constantly looking over the shoulder of the producer and constantly fiddling with what he's doing while he's in the middle of trying to do it. No wonder the producer gets nervous, jumpy, inhibited, and finally can't be coherent. It's an unnecessary burden to try to think of words and also worry at the same time whether they're the right words. (5)

- The same methods don't work to everyone's advantage. Some writers become extremely skillful at completing long, complicated papers in one draft the night before they are due. If everyone is using the same strategy, these students will appear to be the best writers. But such methods work to the disadvantage of many thoughtful, capable writers who need time to consider and reconsider what they have to say. If they resist following the crowd and develop their own approaches, these students often become the best writers in a class.

- For related reasons, if you cling to simple, tidy methods, you will find that as assignments become more challenging, you will become "methodologically challenged": You will appear to be a weak writer and believe that you have reached the limits of your ability, when in fact it is your *approach* to writing that is weak and limited.

All of these limitations relate to the expectations of your teachers, who develop assignments and standards based on their own writing practices. Very few of your teachers can even imagine producing a finished, published article in one draft. Because they have no way of knowing how you produced your assignment, your "patched-up" first draft will suggest to them that this is the best you can do.

Alternatives

In proposing alternatives to the one-draft method, I'm not suggesting that you should simply abandon this approach in favor of another. Because the diverse types of writing assigned in college call for a similar variety of writing strategies, the disadvantages of trying to finish everything in one draft result from *the loss of flexibility in the writing process*, not from the method itself. When an assignment calls for a brief, informal "reaction paper" in response to readings, for example, if you already know what you want to say, you may sensibly choose to complete the paper in one draft. For an important, graded assignment on a complex topic, you will need to consider other strategies, reserving time for research and planning, exploratory writing, and substantial revision. No one method always works for everyone in all types of writing.

If you do not leave your options open and always use the same approach, you will feel vulnerable to these varying demands on your ability. Trying always to make the first draft the last, you will feel you are always on stage, obliged to perform before a potentially critical audience without any rehearsal. Writing for professors, as this sophomore described the experience, can then seem unavoidably stressful and intimidating:

> *Since the majority of my writing is for professors, whom I regard in the beginning as impersonal entities—strangers—I am very insecure about my writing ability. I am constantly conscious of my need to hide my insecurity by writing to meet their approval. Thus, I feel my writing should be coherent, intelligently composed, and interesting in order to reflect some of my nonexistent characteristics.*

This student had become anxious and insecure about her writing because she approached every assignment not as a creative process of learning but as an essay exam—a test of her existing (or "nonexistent") knowledge and ability. Viewed not as performance but as flexible rehearsal time, the writing process offers you many options for bringing "coherent, intelligently composed, and interesting" work into existence, just as you would use rehearsal or "practice" to improve your performance in music, theater, or athletics.

If you thoughtfully adapt your writing methods to particular assignments, this flexibility can offer you great advantages. With the same level of ability as another student who always makes the first draft the last, you can produce better writing, closer to the expectations of your teachers, without spending much additional time if any. You will also get more satisfaction from this work and learn more in the process. Finally, you will have a much wider range of control over your writing in different situations, now and in the future.

The alternatives I propose therefore describe ways of making effective decisions in the process of writing.

As soon as you get an assignment, pause to read it carefully and consider the best strategy for completing it in the time available.   What is your teacher asking you to do, exactly? What kinds of work will a good response to the assignment require, and what are the best times available to do this work?

Start to work on assignments as early as possible. Remember that there is no virtue in delay. If an assignment is due in one week, the best times available to work on it will be distributed throughout that period, and you will greatly reduce your options if you let them pass. Students often behave as though there were some advantage to waiting until the deadline approaches and the pressure builds. They may convince themselves that they write best under pressure, but few writers actually do. Instead, this illusion results from the pressure itself. Because procrastination leaves you little time to reconsider what you are saying, you may write more *quickly* under pressure and feel that this is the best work you can produce under the circumstances. Unable to set your writing aside and return to it from a fresh perspective, you are less likely to observe weaknesses or envision improvements. Under pressure, therefore, you can more easily imagine that a rough draft is a finished product.

In spare moments—walking to class, taking a study break, listening to music—think about the assignment and how you will respond to it. College teachers value thoughtful, interesting responses to assignments. Some of the best ideas occur to us when we are doing something other than sitting at the keyboard, trying to think of something to say. Every new day offers many opportunities for this brief but productive, efficient work on a writing project. Conversations with other students about the assignment can have similar advantages.

In a reflective notebook, keep a record of these ideas as they occur to you. Otherwise, you will quickly forget what you were thinking. If you make informal notes and plans in a specific notebook you carry with you or transfer these ideas to a clearly labeled computer document, when you finally begin to compose a draft, you will have useful material to work with. These informal notes or "reflective journals" are especially helpful in courses that require extensive writing.

Write quick, exploratory drafts of your papers, with low stakes and standards. Whether you produce these informal drafts on paper or on the computer is a matter of individual preference. In either case, if you intend to write further versions and give yourself permission to say *anything* that occurs to you, you can produce a lot of material in a short time. And if you do this exploratory writing well in advance of the due date, you can put it aside for a day or more and come back to it with a fresh perspective, in a better position to reconsider, revise, and organize your ideas.

Between drafts, outline what you have written. You may or may not find it useful to make an outline before you start to compose. That preference also varies from one writer to another. But outlines are equally useful, if not more so, as aids to revision. For that purpose they will reveal the structure of your draft: the connections and disconnections among points, the sequential logic of an argument, gaps, patches of fog, or contradictions. Effective revision can then begin with a revised outline.

Read drafts of your papers aloud, and listen for flow and cohesion. My students tend to *look* for errors and weaknesses in a draft. But our primary orientation to language is through sound, not vision, and we can hear errors, awkward phrasing, and problems of cohesion more accurately than we can see them. As you get better at listening for disruptions in the flow of your writing and trust your ear for these problems, you will be able to listen to the "voice" of the writing without literally reading aloud.

When you read a draft, look for the most important, interesting idea; move it to the beginning; and restructure the paper to follow from it. With surprising frequency, teachers find the best ideas in the middle of papers or toward the end, presented as minor points or afterthoughts. This displacement occurs because the process of writing a draft tends to generate increasingly interesting thoughts about the topic—those that hadn't yet occurred to you when you began to write. If you don't reconsider and revise the structure of your paper, those promising, central ideas will remain buried in later paragraphs as lost opportunities. When you read over your first drafts, therefore, ask the following questions:

> What, and where, is the main idea or argument?
>
> What are the best supporting points for that central idea?
>
> How are these supporting points most logically connected, in a sequence?

Then reorganize your work accordingly, introducing the main point at the beginning and presenting supporting arguments, examples, or evidence in the most logical order.

Do not wait for your teachers to tell you to revise.   Some of your teachers, especially in your writing classes, will give you opportunities to revise papers after you have turned them in, along with suggestions for improvements. But this kind of revision does not eliminate the need for you to revise drafts *before* you turn them in or to make changes beyond those a teacher recommends. Most of us are disappointed when students confine revision to only the changes we suggest, and we are impressed when students take independent responsibility for improving their work.

Do not trust electronic spelling or grammar and style checkers for proofreading.   Because electronic spelling checkers will flag words they do not recognize, they can help you catch many typos and spelling errors when you are proofreading a final draft of your work. But these programs will not reliably identify all of the spelling errors in your writing, partly because they cannot recognize errors that correctly spell other words, such as *to/too* or *there/their*. Checks for grammar and style are much less reliable. Although they will often flag genuine errors, such as missing words or run-on sentences, they will ignore many other types of problems, tell you to revise sentences that are fine the way they are, or even advise you to *make* some kinds of errors. These proofreading systems are most unreliable if you use English as a second language, because they cannot accurately recognize or correct many types of usage and phrasing errors that native speakers of other languages frequently make.

Remember that "the writing" always counts.   Teachers sometimes tell students or give them the impression that they only evaluate "the content" of papers, not "the writing." Don't believe them. They may mean that they don't deliberately look for or mark errors and other problems with structure and style. In an essay or a report, however, *the writing is the content.* Confusing or disconnected arguments and explanations, errors, and poor documentation will always lower the quality of your work, along with your grades.

When you run into trouble, get help.   Most colleges and universities have writing centers that are staffed by teachers or advanced students who can help you to identify and resolve problems in a draft. If your school does not have a writing center, you should use your teacher's office hours to get advice on problems with an assignment, or ask a friend to read through the draft and make suggestions.

None of the preceding options will be available to you, however, if you postpone writing until the night before a paper is due—a common practice through which students unwittingly sacrifice almost all potential for real composure and control over their writing.

Because the mounting pressure to finish an assignment compresses the writing process, reduces options, and forces you to make quick decisions, postponing this work seems most efficient. When procrastination becomes a habit, students often feel that they can write only when they are under pressure, that they can't compose when they feel "composed" or relaxed. But the most successful writers in college eventually recognize the hidden costs of trying to finish everything at the last minute, without time to establish real confidence and control over their work. Like this sophomore, they discover that there are much better ways to use the writing process, with less anxiety and greater satisfaction:

> *There are many different stages to writing, and only one of them involves a finished product. So if I start out, knowing that I am not finished immediately, I have the opportunity to learn and think and truly become engaged in writing. And as I do this, writing becomes less of an external object which inflicts suffering, but a part of me, and something which I can control.*

GUIDELINES

- College teachers observe weaknesses in student papers that *are* characteristic of unrevised first drafts—for example, *unclear theses or arguments, insufficient thought about the topic, poor organization and development,* and *careless proofreading.* These problems typically occur in student papers because they *are* unrevised first drafts.

- You are capable of producing better writing if you use more flexible and effective *methods* of writing.

- The process of writing consists of different types or phases of activity often categorized as prewriting, composing, revising, and editing, prior to the release of writing to its audience (pp. 60–65).

- Although students usually believe that making the first draft the last is the most efficient way to write, this approach is not necessarily efficient and involves some other costs, explained on pp. 71–72.

- If you avoid procrastination and produce exploratory drafts that you intend to revise, you can compose these fairly quickly and, with further reflection and revision, produce much better versions in a reasonable amount of time. You can view other alternative strategies to the one-draft method on pp. 73–77.

5 | Rules and Errors

The person who has acquired knowledge of a language has internalized a system of rules that relate sound and meaning in a particular way. The linguist constructing a grammar of a language is in effect proposing a hypothesis concerning this internalized system.

—Noam Chomsky, *Language and Mind*

Out beyond ideas of wrongdoing and rightdoing,
There is a field. I'll meet you there.

—Jelalluddin Rumi

What Are the Correct Rules for Writing?

We could reasonably expect that questions of right and wrong, and rules and errors, would be the least-confusing aspects of writing, almost by definition. Beneath the many uncertainties of trying to communicate what we want to say to different readers with differing views, expectations, and preferences, the basic rules of grammar and composition, at least, should provide a solid foundation for writing correctly. The belief that native speakers of English should have learned these "basics" of writing in the early years of school (what used to be called grammar school) suggests that these are simple matters of *right* and *wrong*, and *always* and *never*, that we shouldn't need to study further.

As a result of these ideas, you probably feel as a student that all sorts of rules for correct writing are carved in stone—rules that you may remember vaguely but have mostly forgotten. You may imagine that your teachers *do* know all these rules and that they use them both in their own writing and to identify errors in *your* writing when they evaluate your papers. Their comments and corrections tell you what these teachers think is right or wrong, and over the years you have probably used these evaluations to develop, in practice, versions of the rules for writing that you believe teachers want you to follow.

As you move from one grade and course to another, however, these rules sometimes change. New teachers often mark errors that previous teachers ignored, or tell you *not* to do something former teachers told you to do. Types of sentence structure, punctuation, word choice, and organization that were once correct are now incorrect, and some of the "errors" teachers mark on your papers—with comments such as "wrong word" or "weak sentence"—do not violate any of the rules you remember.

College teachers often add to this confusion by maintaining that their students should have learned all of the basics of writing in high school. This expectation would seem reasonable if basic rules and standards for writing remained consistent both between high school and college and throughout the college curriculum.

Having been taught in high school English that you should introduce your thesis with a general discussion, you might receive conflicting instruction from a college teacher that you should "get straight to the point"! What does this mean exactly? Should you *always* get straight to the point when you begin an essay? Should you *always* follow this advice for this subject or for this teacher in this course? Or does that rule apply only to this paper? How can you distinguish real errors—violations of general rules for writing—from matters of preference? Where can you find and learn the *real* rules that all teachers will expect you to follow?

If the essential rules for writing were so simple and clear that you should have learned them years ago, you should also be able to find these rules in a concise book with a title like *The Real Basics of Writing*. No one seems to own a copy of such a book, however, and in the handbooks of grammar and composition available for college students, rules and guidelines are not so simple or clear.

Writing teachers and others who assign writing will probably ask you to buy one of these college handbooks, and in a later section of this chapter and in Chapter 7, I'll explain the best ways to use them most effectively as references. For review of the basics, however, even the most concise, efficient handbooks will look like a maze of rules, guidelines, examples, and exceptions, often presented in technical terms such as *indefinite pronouns* and *predicate nominative*. If you feel that you should remember all this information, negotiating this maze will make you feel ignorant, as if you are failing a grammar test you should have passed in sixth grade. And even the most detailed handbook will not directly explain all the "errors" teachers point out in your papers. If a comment beside a sentence only says "ungrammatical," "awkward," or "unclear," you can't locate the problem in a handbook unless you know enough about sentence structure to identify the problem first; and if you do know this much, you can probably solve the problem on your own.

If you feel uncertain about your grasp of the basics of correct grammar, usage, and style, therefore, I want to assure you that this doubt is completely normal. For teachers and for students, the features of written language that are most often viewed as clear-cut matters of right and wrong or as codes of literary conduct are actually matters of great complexity. Although I can't make these dimensions of writing simple, in the following sections I'll try to reduce the confusion that undermines our efforts to write correctly.

Two Kinds of Rules and Knowledge

Uses of language are not random or unsystematic. They do represent patterns, systems, structures, and rules of various kinds. Like other languages, however, English is a wonderfully complicated, *living* system, generated, maintained, and altered by the diverse people who use it in both writing and speech. Along with perceptions of "correctness," these uses of language change with trends, especially in speech, and they vary among dialects and circumstances.

Noam Chomsky and many other linguists argue that the underlying structures and rules necessary for learning and using any language are built into the human brain; and by all accounts, humans are linguistically brilliant, especially as children. Linguists and grammarians do not create the intricate rules we follow. In the elaborate and subtle uses of our native languages, and of other languages we learn, we are the real experts, and linguists try to understand and systematically *describe* what we are doing with language. Because the linguistic structures and variations we use on a daily basis are so complex, this task is extremely difficult. The *Longman Grammar of Spoken and Written English*, for example, is a 1,200-page description of "systematic patterns of use in English," based on six years of research. Here is a fairly typical sample of the effort to describe detailed rules that writers actually use and their variations—in this case, the use of *to help* with another infinitive, in news and academic writing:

When the verb help *is itself in a* to *clause, a following bare infinitive clause is strongly preferred to a following* to *clause.*

- *In news, 85 percent of all infinitival complement clauses in this context are bare infinitives.*
- *In academic prose and fiction, all infinitival complement clauses in this context are bare infinitives. (737)*

For those of us who are not professional linguists, such explanations are very difficult to follow. (This one simply means that academic writers, especially, avoid the repetition of *to* + verb infinitives, such as *to help to learn*.) But these scholars are trying to explain with analytical precision what the rest of us are doing with English and already know in a different way, much as physiologists try to understand, in terms of functional anatomy, precisely how we walk. We already know how to use these interconnected systems and structures in our lives, even if we don't know their names and can't explain exactly how they work.

To strengthen your formal knowledge of grammar without losing confidence in your own ability, you need to distinguish between two kinds of knowledge and rules, which I call *primary* and *secondary*:

1. *Primary knowledge* is the kind we learn initially through listening and speaking and then through reading and writing in our native languages. The underlying structures and patterns of usage we learn in the process tell us what is correct and represent the rules we actually use to construct sentences, even if we can't explain these rules in linguistic terms. Linguists sometimes call these "internal rules" or "intuitive grammar."

2. *Secondary knowledge* results from the analytical study of grammatical parts and constructions, their names, and the ways they usually work—for example, parts of speech; types of phrases, clauses, and sentences; conjugations of verbs; or the rules that describe agreement between subjects and verbs. This kind of learning—about the ways language works and should work—typically takes place in school.

In your native language, or even as you approach fluency in a foreign language, your ability to write or speak does not depend on this secondary, analytical knowledge of grammar any more than your ability to walk depends on formal knowledge of anatomy. Like anatomical knowledge of the body or ecological knowledge of a familiar environment, however, this second kind of knowledge is extremely useful for solving problems, sharpening perception, learning new languages, and adapting your working knowledge to changing circumstances.

And this distinction between primary and secondary knowledge applies to most kinds of activity and learning. You can't really learn to play tennis or drive a car by reading books about terms and techniques. Through practice and observation, in fact, you can learn to play tennis or drive a car *without* studying terms and techniques. Yet formal knowledge and instruction can help you to learn more quickly, avoid hazards, identify problems, and improve your performance in these activities. Like professional athletes or musicians, accomplished writers continue to refine their technical knowledge of their craft throughout their careers.

"Freewriting" demonstrates, however, that you already possess primary knowledge of language and that you can use this knowledge in writing without the second kind. If you write continuously for a few minutes without pausing to think about what you are going to say, sentences just tumble out onto the page. The writing you produce in this fashion might not be well organized or polished, but you are composing sentences that are connected in passages. You insert periods at the ends of these sentences, and most of you place commas within them where you hear pauses. I know from reading my students' freewriting that most of these sentences and punctuation marks are correct according to the rules contained in handbooks. But how do you know *how* to structure and punctuate these sentences?

In freewriting, you are not pausing to construct sentences deliberately before or while you write them, according to formal rules for grammar and punctuation. To construct a correct sentence, you do not need to think, "I have a singular noun subject for the clause with an adjective modifier, so I should begin with the definite article 'the.' Now I need a present tense verb, and because the subject is a third person singular, I should add an 's' to the end of the verb. This transitive verb will need a direct object. . . ."

In fact, most of you would not be able to think about what you are writing in such detail even if you wanted to, because you have forgotten (or never learned) the linguistic terms and rules that describe the structures of written English. If you *could* think in these complex sentences about writing a sentence, you could just write it, without going through all of this deliberation. And this is what you *are* doing when you compose—with or without technical, linguistic knowledge of grammar. You just write, and sentences come out.

What you are doing is not simple, but the reason you can do it is. Unless you learned English as a second (or third or fourth) language initially through formal instruction, you began to compose complex sentences in speech long before you learned to read or write and long before you began to study grammar in primary school. You acquired this knowledge through listening and speaking, through which you also developed an ear for pauses, breaks, and other inflections. Even if you learned English as a second language, you did not approach fluency through formal knowledge of grammar alone. Becoming fluent means "thinking in" a language, without having to translate words or deliberately assemble sentences.

What does this mean for you as a writer and for your efforts to write correctly? It means your primary, intuitive knowledge of the way English works is generally stronger and more reliable than your secondary, formal knowledge of grammar. For example, you can probably recognize and correct the grammatical error in the following sentence:

Can Noel, the main character in the novel, does whatever he chooses as long as he bears the consequences?

You probably heard that the verb *does* should be changed to *do*, but can you explain *why* you must make that change?

You probably can't, and all the rules you do remember may actually be misleading. A basic rule of subject-verb agreement tells us that if the subject of a verb is a third person singular and the verb is in the present tense, we should add an *s* or *es* to the verb. *Noel* is a third person singular, and *does* is the present tense. Therefore, the construction *Noel does* should be correct, but you know perfectly well that in this sentence it is not. You might guess that this rule doesn't apply if sentences are questions, but the next subject-verb sequences, *he chooses* and *he bears*, do follow the rule.

Even if you eventually figured out that the word *can* (called a "modal auxiliary verb") negates the standard rule for subject-verb agreement within a clause, you could hear and correct the error *before* you could explain it. You could also sense that these two kinds of knowledge are *cognitively different*—that trying to explain what you knew to be an error required a shift to a different kind of thinking.

Proofreading by Ear

Your ear for language is also more reliable than your eye. Or, more accurately, you will notice more when you are not only looking at written language but also *listening* to it. When writers notice errors or awkwardness in a sentence, they typically say that it "sounds wrong," not that it "looks wrong," even if they weren't reading aloud. In fact, it is very difficult to proofread and revise writing effectively without listening to the sound and flow of sentences.

A very large proportion of the errors in student papers are in this sense "typos": mistakes the writers could have caught and corrected if they had read their papers aloud or at least silently vocalized and listened while they proofread. When I ask my students to read their papers aloud, slowly, and listen to the sentences, they can usually catch at least half of the errors they made, and they notice other kinds of problems as well. Sometimes they make the correction or change as they read *before* they notice the problem in the text. Why didn't they notice these problems before they turned in their papers? Because they just "looked over" what they had written, visually scanning the pages with the false assumption that any errors would stand out.

All of us make errors, typos, and awkward sentences while we are writing. One reason is that writing is usually much slower than speech and often broken by pauses that disrupt our sense for the way sentences sound. Reading aloud and listening are therefore especially helpful in punctuating sentences accurately, because most punctuation marks indicate the pauses, breaks, enclosures, and connections among grammatical elements that we hear in speech and want readers to hear in our writing. If you know the *audible* effects of punctuation marks—that commas, for example, create natural pauses within sentences—you can usually *hear* where you need to place them. And if you read this passage from Brian Greene's book *The Fabric of the Cosmos* with all of the punctuation (including capital letters) removed, you will hear the need for punctuation to restore flow and meaning to an unbroken, monotonic string of words:

> *during the first decades of the twentieth century albert einstein made two deep discoveries each caused a radical upheaval in our understanding of space and time einstein dismantled the rigid absolute structures that newton had erected and built his own tower synthesizing space and time in a manner that was completely unanticipated when he was done*

> *time had become so enmeshed with space that the reality of one could no longer be pondered separately from the other.* (39)

With your primary, intuitive knowledge of the grammatical structures of these sentences, you probably know *how* you want to punctuate them as well, without recalling the formal rules that describe your options. Studying the meanings and uses of punctuation marks will certainly help you to make these decisions, which might differ from Greene's without being wrong, but even the most knowledgeable and experienced writers punctuate their work primarily by listening. This is how the passage appears in Greene's book:

> *During the first decades of the twentieth century, Albert Einstein made two deep discoveries. Each caused a radical upheaval in our understanding of space and time. Einstein dismantled the rigid, absolute structures that Newton had erected and built his own tower, synthesizing space and time in a manner that was completely unanticipated. When he was done, time had become so enmeshed with space that the reality of one could no longer be pondered separately from the other.*

Failure to listen to the flow of the writing also caused the structural problem in this sentence from a student paper, which the teacher marked as a grammatical error:

> *It is for this reason that in both "The Purloined Letter" and "The Murders in the Rue Morgue," that Dupin succeeds where the Prefect and the police failed.*

By the time the writer got to the last clause in the sentence, he forgot that he had used "that" in the beginning, and he put in another. If you read the sentence aloud, you can hear the mistake. I'm almost certain that he could have heard it as well and avoided this kind of careless error that substantially lowered his grade.

The value of listening extends beyond the correction of errors to matters of clarity, precision, and style. If this writer had been listening even more closely, he would have noticed that the beginning of the sentence—"It is for this reason that"—sounds a bit cumbersome. If he got rid of "It is" he wouldn't need "that." The sentence would then read as follows:

> *For this reason, in both "The Purloined Letter" and "The Murders in the Rue Morgue," Dupin succeeds where the Prefect and the police failed.*

If he paid even more attention, he might hear a pattern in the way he begins sentences. Here is the first sentence from the next paragraph:

> *It is thinking that separates the successful from the unsuccessful.*

Once again, we find an "It is . . . that" construction at the beginning, and while there is nothing terribly wrong with the sentence, he could recognize the option, at least, of saying it more simply:

> *Thinking separates the successful from the unsuccessful.*

Thinking and listening also separate successful writers from unsuccessful ones.

False Rules

If you trust your ear and just *listen* for the natural pause in the following sentence, you can probably hear that the comma is misplaced:

> *We can view many of O'Keeffe's later paintings as pure abstractions but, all of them were representations of her surroundings.*

In making this common punctuation error, the student was trying to follow the rule that we should *use a comma between two independent clauses joined by a conjunction (such as* and *or* but*) in a compound sentence.* She simply forgot that the comma goes *before* the conjunction, not after, and she didn't listen for the pause.

A large proportion of errors and other problems in student writing result from misguided attempts to follow rules, often on the basis of previous instruction and corrections. In their attempts to be helpful, teachers sometimes point out errors and other problems and refer you to handbooks, online resources, or a writing center for help. In their brief comments and corrections on your papers, however, they can't easily explain *what* is wrong, or *why*, or *how* you can avoid that type of problem in other sentences and papers. Nor do they always distinguish real errors in grammar and usage from ambiguities, stylistic preferences, or particular instances in which a construction doesn't work. As a consequence, student writers often imagine that comments about a specific sentence, paper, or type of writing represent general rules they should *always* follow, and their attempts to follow these "false" rules can create new problems.

For example, when teachers see sentences that have become too long and confusing, they might comment, "Avoid long sentences" or "Run-on sentence," even if the sentence is grammatically correct. When students read this specific comment as general advice, the false rule that they should *always avoid long sentences* may lead them to break up complex statements that must be lengthy to express complex ideas. Their writing can then begin to sound simplistic and choppy, and then another teacher might comment, "Sentences are too short and fragmented," even though these sentences are grammatically complete and not really fragments.

By this time, the writer's own *primary* sense for the diverse ways in which sentences work will be dismantled by two false generalizations and "rules" for writing: (1) *avoid long sentences*, and (2) *avoid short sentences*. Writing sentences can then begin to feel like walking through a minefield of potential errors.

Here are a few of the false rules that my students have told me they learned in high school and tried to follow in college. Although such categories often overlap, I've grouped them roughly as matters of grammar and usage, organization and content, and style:

Grammar and usage

- Don't use the first person (*I* or *we*).
- Don't use the second person (*you*).
- Don't use the passive voice.
- Always use the passive voice in science classes.
- Don't begin a sentence with *because*, *although*, or *unless*.
- Don't begin a sentence with *and* or *but*.
- Don't use more than one *and* in a sentence.
- Don't use contractions.
- Don't use the verb *is*.
- Don't change verb tenses within a paragraph.

Organization and content

- A sentence should contain only one idea.
- A paragraph should contain only one idea.
- Every paragraph should begin with a topic sentence.
- Every paragraph should begin with a transition sentence.
- A paragraph should contain at least two sentences (or three or four).
- A paragraph shouldn't contain more than four sentences (or five or six).
- A thesis statement must come at the end of the first paragraph.

Style

- Show, don't tell.
- Imagine that you are speaking directly to the reader.
- Don't write the way you speak.

I can easily find examples from respectable published writing that contradict these rules, and some of the rules contradict one another. Yet each of them might represent good advice in a particular instance. Clarification therefore requires more elaborate explanations. Here are some examples.

Using the first person. The comment "Don't use the first person" might be valid if you have frequently used the phrase *I think* or *I feel* in an argument based on readings and ideas. If you have chosen to say something, obviously this is what you think, and saying that you "feel" one way or another won't support an argument based on reasoning. The first person is both acceptable and useful, however, when you need to describe your own experiences, actions, or intentions.

Beginning with *because*, *although*. Teachers sometimes tell students not to begin sentences with *because*, *although*, and other subordinating conjunctions when they have written sentence fragments such as *Although the author makes one good point*. Subordinating conjunctions introduce subordinate or dependent clauses and are completely acceptable if their clauses are followed (or preceded) by another, independent clause: *Although the author makes one good point, other parts of her argument are flawed.*

Beginning with *and* or *but*.   *And, but, yet,* and some other small words are called coordinating conjunctions, because they usually link independent clauses, phrases, or words on either side. Beginning a sentence with these words breaks their coordination and sometimes creates fragments, leading some teachers to prohibit this practice. But occasionally (as in this sentence), if you want to emphasize the break, you can begin with a coordinating conjunction—even with an emphatic sentence fragment: *But not always.*

Using *is*.   Excessive use of *is* and other forms of the verb *to be* can deaden your writing, because verbs enliven sentences by indicating particular kinds of action, intention, and connection between subjects and objects. In description, for example, forms of the linking verb *to be* simply tell us things are there and have certain characteristics:

> *The room **is** large. There **is** a door in the middle of one wall. There **is** also a window. There **are** two bookshelves.*

Other verbs help to establish connections and spatial relations in longer, more fluent sentences:

> *The door in the middle of one wall **opens** into a large room, with a window **flanked** by bookshelves in the opposite wall.*

It is almost impossible, however, to avoid all uses of *to be*, partly because they combine with other verbs to form passives (*is told*), progressives (*are running*), and other necessary expressions.

Limiting ideas in a sentence or paragraph.   Because *ideas* and *topics* come in all sizes, it is impossible to dictate how many a sentence, paragraph, or essay should contain. A teacher might tell you for good reasons that you should divide a long paragraph with two main ideas. But even some long *sentences* relate two ideas, and a paragraph might present three or more ideas as subtopics of its central theme. You will observe that paragraphs in published work vary greatly in length, from one sentence to ten or more, depending on their functions within the work as a whole.

Placing the thesis statement.   As I've mentioned in previous chapters, the beginning of an essay should establish an understanding of what the writing is about, along with a sense of direction. In academic writing, a *thesis statement, central question,* or *definition of a problem* usually appears early in the work—often at the end of the introductory paragraph or section. If you examine published essays or magazine articles, however, you will find that central theses or questions do not always land at the end of the first paragraph. They might appear at the very beginning or in later paragraphs. The beginning of an essay might pose a question that is answered only at the end, with a particular argument or conclusion.

Showing or telling. *Showing* usually means illustrating with examples and descriptions; *telling* usually means explaining or discussing. Most kinds of academic writing require both, their proportions depending on the type and purpose of the writing. A case study or autobiographical essay might consist largely of narration and description. An argument about ideas might consist largely of explanation, with a few examples used for support or clarification. The introduction and discussion sections of a scientific report *tell* us what the experiment is about and why it is important. The methods and results sections, including figures, *show* us how the experiment was done and the results it produced. In academic writing you might need to alter the proportions of showing and telling, but you cannot avoid either of these modes of presentation altogether.

Writing versus speaking. Writing always retains some relation to speech, and to write well, you must maintain a sense for the way your "writing voice" will sound to readers. Formal writing will sound like formal speech; informal writing will sound more like conversation. These writing voices will be appropriate or inappropriate for specific occasions and audiences, just as styles of speech you use with your friends will be inappropriate for an interview with an employer. When teachers tell you not to "write the way you speak," therefore, they usually mean that you have used chatty, colloquial styles that are not suitable for academic writing, not that you should sever all of the essential connections between writing and speech.

Most false rules therefore result from our tendency to turn local advice into general principles—to read "in this case" to mean "always" or "never." Because both teachers and students wish writing were less complicated than it is, we look for ways to make it simpler—more reliably successful. If your teachers notice a pattern of usage that gets you into trouble, it's hard for them to resist telling you to avoid that pattern. If teachers find a way to avoid common errors or weaknesses in your writing, they will often prescribe that method. And when someone tells you that something is wrong in your paper, you will try to avoid that construction in *all* of your papers to reduce the risk of further criticism or poor grades. Yet each time you turn local advice into a general rule, you narrow your range of choices and undermine your intuitive sense for the subtle ways in which language works or doesn't work in particular instances.

In fact, the majority of the comments that refer to writing style and structure in returned papers point out specific problems in specific sentences, often with a single word or abbreviation. When I examine papers that teachers have returned to students, I find many comments like these:

awkward sentence (awk)	unclear (unc)	vague
wrong word (ww)	diction	wordy
unnecessary	redundant	syntax?
grammar (gr)	rambling	organization (org)
logic?	evidence?	

In many cases, teachers place question marks beside underlined sentences or simply circle words and phrases, indicating that *something* is wrong. Other comments, such as *Is this true?*, refer to particular statements the writer has made, the way those statements were phrased, or contradictions between statements in different parts of the essay.

Rules will not tell you what is wrong in these instances. Instead, question marks, circles, and underlining, like many brief comments in the margins, indicate that the teacher wants you to read over and reconsider what you said or the way you said it. For example, a teacher simply underlined the following sentence, put brackets around some of the words, and wrote "rephrase" in the margin:

> *This knowledge [brings a] transformation [to the psychology of] Douglass from a simple slave to a complex thinker.*

This sentence does not violate any rules I can think of. What was this teacher noticing about it? What exactly did she want the writer to do? If you read the sentence aloud, you can probably hear that it sounds a bit awkward, or "wordy." The brackets suggest that the words within them can be eliminated. How can you change the sentence to make it sound more direct and concise? The most obvious solution changes the noun "transformation" into a verb, eliminating the words in brackets:

> This knowledge transforms Douglass from a simple slave to a complex thinker.

If you can't figure out on your own what your teacher has noticed and wants you to do (or if the comments aren't legible), ask the teacher to explain or go to the writing center on your campus and get help from its staff.

How to Use a Handbook

Because they can't explain most errors and other problems in brief comments, teachers may ask you to buy a specific handbook of grammar and composition and refer you to relevant sections. Other teachers will assume that you own one of these books and will use it for review and reference. Most of the college handbooks available in print also offer electronic versions for convenient access while you are working on your computer, and some have companion Web sites.

Unlike the massive works such as the *Longman Grammar*, college handbooks do not attempt to describe all uses and variations of English. Instead, authors of handbooks try to anticipate the kinds of information college students will need, and they organize this material with index tabs and other keys that help you find relevant sections. Before you use a handbook, therefore, you should spend a couple of minutes examining its overall structure. Some recent college handbooks begin with sections that tell you how to find information and use the book most efficiently.

If you do not own one of these reference books, I recommend that you buy one of the concise, spiral-bound varieties designed for college students and for quick reference. Two of the most popular handbooks of this type are *A Writer's Reference*, 6th ed., by Diana Hacker (Bedford/ St. Martin's, 2007) and *Keys for Writers*, 4th ed., by Ann Raimes (Houghton Mifflin, 2004).

Many teachers and students now prefer the smaller "pocket" versions of handbooks, because they are more portable and inexpensive than full-sized handbooks and writing guides. These little references will retain most of the essential information you need on mechanics and documentation, with shorter explanations, fewer examples, and very little guidance on composition.

College handbooks contain three kinds of information: (1) general guidance for writing; essays; (2) guidance for completing and documenting research papers; and (3) sections on the "mechanics" of grammar, sentence structure, punctuation, and style. In addition, recent handbooks contain sections on using Internet sources and, as I'll discuss in the following section, limited advice for students who use English as a second language (ESL). Because linguistic terms are to some extent unavoidable in the explanation of grammar and syntax, most include glossaries of these terms.

Diana Hacker's *A Writer's Reference* offers a concise section on "Basic Grammar," designed for writers who want a quick review of the parts of speech and the types of phrases, sentences, and clauses. This review will make it easier for you to locate and understand more detailed explanations of specific constructions. Her Web site, called "Rules for Writers," http://bcs.bedfordstmartins.com/rules6e/Player/pages/main.aspx, offers expanded explanations and exercises in grammar, research, documentation, ESL problems, and other aspects of student writing.

I'm often surprised to learn that my students don't own a handbook of grammar and composition or that they avoid using the one they do own. Some have told me that reading about grammar and rules makes them feel stupid—that a handbook reminds them of tests, errors, and everything they should have learned back in elementary school. That's unfortunate, because a handbook—like a dictionary, an almanac, or a telephone directory—just provides convenient reference to information we *can't* remember. That's what reference books are for.

However, you can think of a handbook of English as an owner's manual. You are the real owner of the language it describes. An *Owner's Manual of Written English* just helps you to understand how your language is structured, how you can use it most effectively, and how to fix problems.

In Chapter 7, for example, I'll emphasize the convenience of using a handbook for citing and documenting sources in research papers. No one expects you to remember all of the details for documenting different kinds of sources consistently within a particular system. (I certainly can't remember them.) Handbooks clearly sort out the documentation formats for books, articles, and other kinds of sources with examples, so if you need to document a newspaper article or an essay in an edited collection, you can easily find the correct form in the system you are using. Other sections show you how to integrate and cite quotations in the text of your research paper and the general format for a list of references, or "Works Cited," at the end.

Handbooks are more difficult to use for solving particular structural problems in your papers, unless your teacher has clearly identified the problem or referred you to a specific section of the book. Beside this description of people at a carnival, for example, a teacher might write "unparallel" or ≠:

> *Most of them were stuffing their faces with ice cream cones, popcorn, hot dogs, or smoking cigarettes.*

If you look up *parallelism* in the index to your handbook, you will find a section that describes this kind of structural and stylistic error, which creates the impression in this case that people were devouring lit cigarettes.

Beside the following sentence, a teacher might write, "comma splice" or "run-on." Or you might find that the comma is circled, perhaps with a semicolon in its place:

> *Gribner believes he is making arguments about race, however the statistics he uses as evidence represent social and economic class.*

If you look up *comma splice, run-on sentences, commas,* or *semicolons* in the index of your handbook, all of these terms will help you identify one of the most common errors in student writing: the use of a comma to splice together two independent clauses that could stand as separate sentences. Writers frequently use commas incorrectly before words such as *however, moreover,* and *therefore* because they think these words are conjunctions like *and* or *but*. In fact, these are conjunctive adverbs that are often used to introduce independent clauses. As a consequence, the comma is an error—a comma splice—and the standard punctuation in this case is a semicolon.

The effort to solve problems in your own writing is usually the best way to review grammar, sentence structure, and punctuation—features of the language that are almost always related. Because a large proportion of the errors in student writing involve punctuation, however, *I strongly recommend that you review the entire punctuation section in a college handbook*, with particular attention to the basic functions and effects of punctuation marks. Student writers tend to avoid, confuse, and misuse marks such as the semicolon, colon, and dash, as though these were hopelessly mysterious, complicated forms of punctuation. But the rules and functions of these marks are actually very easy to learn—much easier than the diverse rules for using commas, for example—by studying about two pages of a handbook for each of them. Usually confined to thirty pages or fewer, the punctuation sections of handbooks are the most efficient and valuable points of departure for the review of grammar and sentence structure.

As you begin to locate explanations for specific problems in your writing, you can also let one section lead you to others in an exploratory fashion. In the previous example of the comma splice, the definition of that error will invite you to review the types of clauses. In another section you will find a definition and lists of conjunctive adverbs used in this kind of sentence. If you wonder why a semicolon works in this sentence, whereas a comma does not, turn to the section on semicolons. You can easily find all of these terms in the index or key to the contents of your handbook. One sentence can therefore direct the review of substantial areas of grammar, syntax, and punctuation.

A Note to Nonnative Speakers of English

While I was considering changes for this edition of *The Transition to College Writing*, I sought advice from members of an unusually diverse, international freshman writing class, most of whom had learned English as a second or third language. One of these students recommended that I should include, as some writing texts do, special advice for "ESL" (English as a Second Language) students in each chapter, perhaps in boxed sections.

To my surprise, most of the other students disagreed. "I don't think we belong in separate boxes," one of them argued. "Our problems aren't *that* different."

Because there are no boxed ESL sections in this edition, I've obviously sided with the majority of this class. But the complex issue they raised is important for all of us in higher education, and I appreciate both sides of the debate. Nonnative speakers of English *do* need and deserve special kinds of help in learning to use academic English effectively, and in this section I'll briefly describe the kinds of resources available for these purposes. These needs and resources vary considerably, however, and in this small volume I can't fully describe, much less provide, the kinds of instruction necessary to solve the diverse problems that uses of academic English pose for students with different language backgrounds and levels of English fluency.

The main lesson I've learned from teaching at an increasingly international, multicultural university, furthermore, is that individual students do not fit neatly into categories of any kind. The attempt to fit ESL advice into "separate boxes" would falsely suggest that those of you who use English as a second or foreign language are categorically *different* from native speakers of English and that you are categorically *alike*. Because these generalizations are false, they can undermine your efforts to identify and solve the *specific* problems of adjustment you face—problems you may share with many native speakers of English and those you will not share, in particular cases, with other ESL students.

Realistically assessing your individual strengths, weaknesses, and needs is especially difficult at the beginning of college studies, when all new students are more or less disoriented and worried about their prospects for success. Responding to a survey that one of my classes conducted, first-term freshmen reported that compared to the abilities of their peers, on average they believed they were *below* average! In the following months, the most confident students often run into the most trouble, and those who thought they were heading for disaster (after receiving a low grade on a paper or exam) often flourish.

At the beginning of college, therefore, even minor difficulties with English can make you feel generally disadvantaged in comparison to other students, most of whom are coming to false conclusions about their own abilities. Initial struggles to learn English at more basic levels in a foreign culture—in a state of "culture shock"—can make academic survival seem impossible at first. A student who came to college directly from Hong Kong found American English so disorienting that she couldn't understand lectures, didn't speak a full sentence in English for two weeks, and nearly abandoned her studies. At the beginning of the following year, I learned that she was an orientation counselor for incoming freshmen.

Because the new students who converge on particular campuses must adapt to the same educational environments and expectations, the advice offered in this chapter and others is addressed to all of you who are entering college, regardless of your diverse linguistic and cultural backgrounds. As ESL students, you may feel categorically disadvantaged because you imagine that native speakers of the language are, by definition, entirely fluent in English. In their uses of *academic*

English in college, however, they are not. If you listen to casual conversations among college students, for example, these will not sound like the language used in lectures and readings in your courses. Academic English is a particular *dialect*, or assortment of dialects, that is very different from the ones most students speak.

While learning to use academic English effectively at the college level, therefore, students from all types of language backgrounds run into these difficulties:

- They make structural and stylistic errors.

- They have difficulties with the organization and development of their written work.

- They enter college with limited working vocabularies and must learn a lot of new terms to grasp central concepts and express themselves effectively in particular fields of study.

- In writing or in class discussions, they often feel they must translate their thoughts into unfamiliar terms and forms of expression.

To the extent that we can identify "ESL problems" with academic English, these do not represent categories of difficulty separate from the preceding ones. Within these categories, instead, as individual nonnative speakers of English, you will make particular *kinds* of errors for *reasons* that will be mostly linked with differences (or in some cases similarities) between your native languages and English. And these problems will have different implications and solutions in the development of your language skills. Your working vocabulary in English may be considerably weaker than in your native language, and for this reason "translation" from thought to expression in English can have different implications as well.

However, some of your strengths and weaknesses, in using English, and in academic work more generally, may be identical to those of many native speakers of English or may have applied equally to work in your native languages and cultures. Although international experience and knowledge of other languages can create initial difficulties of adjustment, these same factors can become great assets in your college studies and careers.

For reasons I'll soon explain, experienced writing teachers and ESL specialists can give you the clearest and most constructive help in identifying your individual abilities and needs. But other teachers, without specialized training in language instruction, will also evaluate your work and give you advice about areas that need improvement. To avoid confusion, you should be aware of the potential value and limitations of their assessments.

What You Can (and Can't) Expect from Teachers

In their own fields and professional lives, at least, college teachers *are* native speakers and writers of academic English. Their uses of language and evaluations therefore represent the standards to which all college students must try to conform. Ideally, then, their comments, corrections, and other evaluations of your written work should clearly and consistently tell you the ways your own uses of language do *not* conform to established standards for academic writing, in general and in that field of study.

As I've observed in previous sections of this chapter, however, individual teachers have differing standards and preferences. In addition, space and time limit the amounts and types of feedback teachers can give you on returned papers. In relation to their own sense for the way writing *should* work, they may point out what works and does not work in your writing. But those who are not professional language teachers can rarely explain the relative importance of particular errors and other problems, why those problems occurred, and how you can solve them.

These limitations apply to all student writers, and they explain the main purposes of specialized writing instruction: to answer questions about *relative importance, why,* and *how*. It's especially difficult for teachers who are not trained in language instruction to understand the relative importance, causes, and solutions for ESL errors and related difficulties. Their responses to your writing can therefore be very different and potentially confusing. A teacher in one class might ignore these problems and focus entirely on the substance of your writing. Another might circle or underline incorrect words or phrases or simply note that such errors exist. And occasionally, a teacher might consider minor errors to be serious obstacles to communication, even in writing that is otherwise clear and fluent.

For example, here is a passage from a returned paper about a bronze sculpture that was written by a college freshman whose native language is Cantonese. The underlined words are those the teacher marked as errors, with changes indicated in bold parentheses:

> *Even though the artist's sculpture seems to be a figure outside of soci-*
> *ety, ironically, the artist did not keep the natural color of the bronze;*
> *the sculpture have̲ (has) paint over it. In t̶h̶e̶ society, t̶h̶e̶ appearance is*
> *important, and ironically the artist painted the bronze. The exact reason*
> *is unknown, but I think the artist is trying to say that t̶h̶e̶ appearance is*
> *important whether i̲t̲ (what?) is outside or within the society.*

In the margin beside this passage, the teacher drew lines to the three uses of the word "the" and noted, "gr. You have trouble with the use of the definite article in English." Almost all of the other corrections and comments on this paper also identified specific errors in the use of articles, prepositions, verb forms, or phrasing that stood out to this teacher as what he termed, in his final comment, "serious ESL problems." He was so distracted by these errors, in fact, that he ignored the more substantial problem of repetition in the passage: that the first two sentences make essentially the same statement twice in similar language.

This teacher was functioning essentially as a proofreader for errors, and this kind of thorough correction, if it reveals patterns, can be useful to you in developing your own proofreading skills. The message that these local errors represent "serious ESL problems," however, is not an accurate, helpful assessment of their significance or of the writer's level of fluency in English. The specific errors he marked—in the use of articles and prepositions and in subject-verb agreement in number (as in "the sculpture have")—are among the last obstacles to fluency for native speakers of many Asian languages. In themselves, they do not indicate that the writer lacks basic knowledge of English grammar and sentence structure. Instead, these and other lingering difficulties with English remain because (1) *they cannot be easily explained or corrected with reference to rules*, and (2) *they represent structural differences between your native language and English.*

Here lies the potential cause of confusion. Some teachers imagine that such errors result from a lack of "basic" knowledge of English grammar because native speakers of English do not tend to make these errors.

If you recently learned English primarily through formal study of grammar and sentence structure, however, you may know consider-ably *more* about rules and constructions than most native speakers of English do.

We can account for this apparent contradiction by looking at the two kinds of knowledge: primary and secondary (these are defined on

p. 82). Native speakers of English learn how to use articles, prepositions, complex verb forms, and hundreds of "idiomatic" expressions (particular ways of saying things) initially through primary speaking and listening, not through the study of grammar and usage, and they can rarely explain these patterns of usage in linguistic, secondary terms. For the same reason, these are the most difficult features of English for nonnative speakers to master, because you cannot master them completely through rules and the study of grammar.

Complete fluency in a language always results from the development of primary knowledge as well: an increasingly accurate sense for the way particular uses of the language should *sound*. If you have learned to rely on your knowledge of grammar, therefore, to increase your fluency, like other writers you will also need to develop, use, and trust your ear for the sound and flow of fluent sentences. In addition to the specialized resources I'll discuss, you can make substantial progress on your own or with limited help from writing teachers and other students by doing the following:

- Read drafts of your work aloud, and *listen* for errors, poor word choices, and other disruptions to the sound and flow of sentences. If you can find someone to read your work to you, you can look at a copy while listening more attentively.

- When teachers point out patterns of error, and as you notice them on your own, make a list of these problems to watch for when you proofread and revise your work.

- When you have identified lingering patterns of error in your writing or in speech, notice how these constructions work in the academic writing you read. Extensive reading, in general, is extremely important for building intuitive knowledge and vocabulary.

- Speak English as much as possible. Some schools have large communities of students who also speak your native language, and it may seem both easier and more natural to speak that language with them. Keep in mind, however, that the speed with which you develop English language skills and adapt to college more generally will result directly from your use of English in speaking as in writing and reading.

- If your school sponsors a peer or staff tutoring service, bring drafts of your papers to these tutors for advice and instruction.

In the process, individual teachers' evaluations of your writing can give you potentially useful, if differing, information about the qualities they value in writing, about the strengths and weaknesses they observe in your work. Even so, if you feel that their evaluations of your work are confusing or unfair, it's extremely important for you to clarify these issues as early as possible in your college studies.

- If you are sufficiently fluent in English that you do not need specialized ESL instruction, you can still ask professional writing and ESL instructors to assess samples of your writing and recommend ways of improving areas of weakness.

- If you are taking a general writing class, ask your teacher for advice about difficulties you are having with writing in other courses as well. Students are often reluctant to do this, but writing teachers are concerned about your performance on written work in all of your classes.

- If you feel that you are being penalized in a course for lingering errors you can't reliably correct on your own, talk with your teacher about your concerns and explain the nature of your difficulties.

Special Resources for Nonnative Speakers of English

Institutional resources for ESL students vary considerably among colleges and universities, depending on their size and the linguistic diversity of their student populations. But the great majority of schools do have systems for identifying and assisting incoming students who need special help in reaching fluency in English. These systems include consideration of application materials such as standardized test scores and writing samples, writing assessment and placement tests when students arrive, and referrals from freshman writing instructors and other faculty. Writing centers often include instructional materials and tutoring services designed for nonnative speakers of English, and some schools sponsor peer tutoring or mentoring programs that pair native speakers of English with ESL students for conversation and help with written English.

If you are an international student, your school will probably consider your TOEFL (Test of English as a Foreign Language) scores as an initial basis for determining the kinds of instruction you need, often followed by assessments of writing samples and individual conferences.

For ESL students whose citizenship or residency status does not require the TOEFL, there are usually comparable assessment procedures. If you are having significant trouble with writing, reading, or speaking in English and were not assessed, you should locate the people who run these programs and let them know about your difficulties. Faculty advisers, international student offices, and the staff of writing centers may be able to help you with this process.

Small schools may have only one level of ESL instruction. Large ESL programs may offer a wide variety of specialized courses for students at different levels of fluency in English and with different kinds of language backgrounds, including courses that emphasize conversational and public speaking or academic reading in addition to writing. If your school does not offer ESL courses and related services, you may be able to find comparable instruction in the surrounding community.

If you need at least one semester of ESL instruction, your difficulties with English comprehension and expression may include the following:

- Limited vocabulary and *working* knowledge of grammar and sentence structure in English

- Related problems with reading speed and comprehension

- Reliance on translation to and from your native languages, with extensive help from bilingual dictionaries

- Struggles to express complex thoughts in English in complex sentences

- Low confidence in your spontaneous ability to produce sentences that make sense to native speakers of English

- Reluctance, therefore, to engage in class discussions, conferences with teachers, or conversations in English, with a resulting sense of linguistic isolation

For reasons I've explained, teachers who are not trained in ESL instruction can rarely provide substantial help in these areas, which require specialized knowledge of the differences among languages and of the ways in which people learn foreign languages, with materials and activities designed for this kind of teaching.

If you are recommended or required to take ESL classes, you should think of this instruction as an important benefit your school provides to hasten your adjustment and contribute to your success in college, not as a punishment or delay in your studies. If you do not need to take ESL classes, you may still benefit from other courses, services, and instruction materials available for nonnative speakers of English at higher levels of fluency. Courses and services may include developmental writing courses; peer tutoring programs; workshops on academic reading, oral communication, study skills, or specific ESL problems; and consultations with writing center or ESL staff.

Because the college handbooks I described in this chapter are designed primarily for native speakers of English, they will offer very limited help with the complex and "unruly" areas of grammar and usage that probably give you the most trouble, such as problems with articles and prepositions. Many of these problems concern the specific ways words are used in phrases and sentences, so a large dictionary can give you some guidance. Look especially for a dictionary that includes sample sentences, plural forms of nouns, conjugations of verbs, and distinctions between transitive and intransitive verbs (usually indicated by abbreviations such as *v.i.* and *v. int.*).

For nonnative speakers of English, one specialized dictionary that emphasizes the ways words are used and supplies many examples is *The BBI Combinatory Dictionary of English: A Guide to Word Combinations*, published by John Benjamins Publishing Company (1986).

In addition, many grammar handbooks, textbooks, and workbooks focus on the features of grammar and usage that are most troubling to nonnative speakers of English. The "Rules for Writers" Web site (see p. 94) includes a section of ESL exercises, and you can find many helpful exercises on the most troublesome patterns of grammar and usage for ESL students in *Understanding and Using English Grammar*, by Betty Azar (Prentice-Hall, 2001). Three concise grammar texts that are very useful as reference books are *Grammar Troublespots: A Guide for Student Writers*, by Ann Raimes (Cambridge University Press, 2004); *Longman Student Grammar of Spoken and Written English*, by Douglas Biber et al. (Pearson Education, 2002); and *A Practical English Grammar*, by A. J. Thompson and A. V. Martinet (Oxford, 1986).

If you are having difficulty with English comprehension and expression, however, the most important key to your development is *practice* in using English freely, with confidence that you can overcome these problems with support from teachers and fellow students. Reluctance to speak and write out of fear of making errors can be the most serious obstacle to your satisfaction and success as college students, regardless of your language skills and backgrounds. College teachers are usually more concerned about students who remain silent than they are about students who make errors and explain their difficulties. One reason is that teachers can help the latter students but not the former. Another reason is that college teachers value differences among their students and want everyone to participate in the exchange of ideas. A college or university is a wonderful mixture of people from diverse backgrounds, very few of whom are native inhabitants of higher education or native speakers of academic English. All of you contribute to this rich collection of languages and dialects, cultures, and ideas; through open communication and interaction, all of you can benefit from this richness as well.

GUIDELINES

- Although teachers often describe concerns with grammar, rules, and errors as the "basics" of writing, these dimensions of language are extremely complex, and the "rules" that teachers expect students to know often change.

- To avoid confusion about the rules of English and what we are actually doing as writers, we need to distinguish two kinds of rules and knowledge of language:
  - *Primary knowledge* learned through the use of language, initially through listening and speaking, then through reading and writing as well
  - *Analytical knowledge*, with which linguists attempt to describe regular structures and patterns of usage

- Your primary knowledge of the way English works is generally stronger and more reliable than your secondary, analytical knowledge of grammar.

- Your ear for language is also more reliable than your eye. This means you can usually hear more errors and other problems in your work by reading it aloud than you can see by "looking over" a draft.

- A large proportion of the errors student writers make results from their efforts to follow false rules. Many of these false rules about grammar, organization, and style were initially false generalizations derived from specific comments, such as "Don't use the first person" (pp. 87–93).

- Handbooks of grammar are essentially reference books—like owner's manuals—best used for solving specific problems in your own writing and understanding how specific features of the language work.

- In terms of their language abilities and difficulties, nonnative speakers of English do not represent a separate category of college students. Because all students must adapt to academic English and unfamiliar environments, nonnative speakers of English simply face some different challenges of adjustment that often require special kinds of assistance.

- College teachers who are not trained to teach writing or ESL usually have a limited ability to understand and evaluate ESL difficulties. While they may be able to point out *what* is wrong, they can rarely explain the relative importance of those problems, why they occur, or how you can solve them.

- If you have serious difficulties with comprehension and expression in English, therefore, you will need specialized instruction in the use of English as a second or foreign language. Some common indications of this need for ESL instruction are listed on page 103.

6 Footstools and Furniture

Variations of Form and Flow in College Writing

> The biggest change that occurred in my experience with college writing was learning how to write for a variety of subjects. In high school the majority of the papers that I had to write were for English classes. This normally involved writing analytical papers on novels. In college, I had to learn how to change my writing style according to the different types of subject matter. College writing allows the writer a chance to be versatile. Becoming a versatile writer was a big adjustment for me.
>
> — A College Sophomore

What's Wrong with the "Footstool Essay"?

The one-draft method described in Chapter 4 would be more reliable (and your lives as student writers much simpler) if there were also one form of writing—one way of organizing information and ideas—that would work for every assignment you received in college. If such an all-purpose template for structuring papers existed, writing would resemble filling in the blank spaces in a standardized form. You would still have to figure out what to say in those spaces, but before you even started to write, you would have a basic plan.

In middle school or high school, many of you learned to use an all-purpose essay format, perhaps in preparation for taking standardized essay exams. And college teachers, especially in freshman writing classes, are very familiar with this predictable form of writing, which has been taught with varying consistency in American schools for several decades. "As a writer in high school," one college freshman recalled in a slightly macabre way, "I was told to follow a certain formula, introducing the topic with an introduction, concluding with a conclusion, and filling the space in between with a body."

To explain to my students why such formulas no longer work in college, even though some of their principles may remain useful, I often use the following analogy:

> Imagine that you have learned basic woodworking skills by perfecting the construction of a good footstool. Although footstools themselves have limited uses, your instructor has chosen this task to teach you fundamental principles and skills: the selection of materials, the use of tools, methods of shaping and joining parts, and techniques for polishing the finished product.
>
> Now suppose that you move on from this training to a job as an apprentice in a large furniture factory, where you move from one department to another, for exposure to the full range of products and operations. Among these departments, many of the tools, materials, and procedures are familiar to you, but they are used to construct a great variety of products. Some have legs and tops, like a footstool, but some do not, and there are also unfamiliar parts and procedures: drawers, doors, and shelves, hinges and pulls, dovetail or mortise and tenon joints, different glues and dowels for different purposes, and various finishes for different styles of furniture. Some of these styles are highly ornate and creative, whereas others are plain and functional. Your supervisors in these departments have different standards for "good" furniture and different expectations for your work. The challenges are bewildering and, although your early training is useful for these diverse tasks, no one asks you to build a footstool.
>
> "Don't get discouraged," an experienced worker reassures you. "Eventually you'll pass through this stage and settle into one kind of job. For now, just pay attention and learn as much as you can." Indeed, as the range of your experience expands, you gradually become better at adapting the skills you have already acquired to new tasks. Yet none of this development could occur until you stopped making footstools.

The footstool in this analogy is sometimes called the five-paragraph theme or the keyhole essay, the latter term coined many years ago by Sheridan Baker in a popular writing text titled *The Practical Stylist.* According to this formula, the introduction should take the shape of a funnel, beginning with a broad statement of the topic and narrowing to a thesis statement at the end. This statement lists the subtopics, or "points," of the following paragraphs, and the body of the essay raises these points in order. The final paragraph should begin somewhat narrowly, perhaps as a reiteration of the thesis, and broaden in the form of an inverted funnel to some kind of conclusion. The typical choice of three supporting points, plus the introduction and conclusion, accounts for the term *five-paragraph theme*, and *keyhole* roughly describes the overall shape of the essay, which my students often diagram this way:

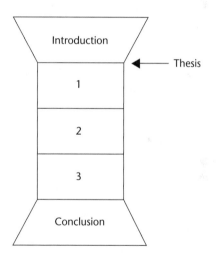

High school teachers often use some version of this formula to prepare students for the AP English exam and other timed assessments of writing ability because it provides a structure for writing a brief essay on almost any subject. Whether you are writing arguments, summaries, explanations, or comparisons, on the causes of a war, the advantages of managed health care, or the duties of a citizen, this model allows you to begin with a basic outline. Once you have identified a central thesis and three supporting points or subcategories, you know that you should begin with some general observations about the topic, narrow the introduction to a topic sentence that lists your supporting points, discuss these points in order in the body paragraphs of the essay, return to your thesis in the conclusion, and end with further generalization. If you "say what you are going to say, say it, and say you've said it" (as some teachers instruct their students), neither the writer nor the reader can possibly get lost. If you follow these simple instructions, your essay should turn out right every time—like a cake mix.

Individual students learn, or develop, many variations of this formula on their own. I knew a college freshman who *always* began her essays with a quotation from some well-known author, which she used to introduce the general theme of the paper and three subtopics, discussed in following paragraphs. A college junior realized that the prescription for "good" writing that he learned in his senior year of high school was really a prescription for getting through the Advanced Placement English test:

> At the time, I believed that what I was learning were the "laws" of writing that every college student everywhere used to write effective papers. It is true that what I had learned worked perfectly for my specific purpose; it was exactly the style the Advanced Placement test-givers and my instructor wanted and encouraged. Although the style and rules that I learned are not totally useless (I use them sometimes to give my writing organization and direction if it is straying), they had negative consequences on style and creativity.
>
> For some reason unbeknownst to me, many of the rigid rules I observed had to do with the number three.
>
> Rule #1: Each paragraph should have at least three sentences.
>
> Rule #2: There should be at least three paragraphs to the body of a composition.
>
> Rule #3: The writer should strive to have three forms of proof or evidence for each of the three supporting ideas of the thesis.

You can observe some of the unfortunate effects of such formulas on "style and creativity" in the following writing assessment essay, which was written by an entering college freshman who was asked to "discuss factors that facilitate or hinder learning":

> In order for people to learn, there must be a good learning atmosphere. Many things can affect the atmosphere in which people try to learn.

> *Some of them are class sizes, stress, and the professor's way of teach-*
> *ing. A bad learning atmosphere hinders learning because people can't*
> *concentrate and absorb the material to be learned.*
>
> *Large classes hinder learning. Large classes cause the student to*
> *get less individual student-professor contact. They also put the student*
> *farther from the teacher so it's harder to focus on him/her. The student*
> *would have a greater distance between him/her and the front of the*
> *room where the professor is speaking.*
>
> *Stress from outside of class hinders learning. Stress also could distract*
> *students in class by giving them other things to think about. It might*
> *also cause headaches that would hinder or prevent proper concentra-*
> *tion. If students have large amounts of stress, it messes up sleeping*
> *patterns. This could cause students to fall asleep in class or be too tired*
> *to learn properly. Stress hinders learning because of the effect it has on*
> *both the mind and the body.*
>
> *Professors who speak in a language only they can understand hinder*
> *learning. Students then spend too much time trying to figure out what*
> *the professors are saying. This causes the students to not be able to take*
> *proper notes. Students might also lose interest in the class that is needed*
> *for them to survive. Students might continue to fall below an ever in-*
> *creasing pile of work as they try to understand. Students' ability to learn*
> *is hindered when professors speak in a language only the professors can*
> *comprehend.*
>
> *Learning is hindered when the atmosphere isn't conducive to learning.*
> *This happens when the student has too many stresses outside of class. It*
> *also happens when students are in large classes because students don't*
> *get as much contact with the professor. Professors who speak in a lan-*
> *guage only they can understand hinder learning because the students try*
> *to understand them instead of the material. The atmosphere of the class-*
> *room is hindering learning when things such as these occur.*

This is a particularly rigid, skeletal example of a "five-paragraph theme,"
but I suspect that the student who wrote it believed that he was doing
exactly what he should do to demonstrate to college teachers that he
could write a well-organized essay.

The teachers who evaluated the essay, however, considered it the
work of a weak writer who might not be able to meet the demands of
college work. The way this writer used the five-paragraph formula made

his essay seem an empty formality rather than a thoughtful response to the question. It is very obvious that the writer is simply manufacturing an introduction and a conclusion and "filling the space in between with a body," severed into three parts. Paragraphs consist of flat, disconnected statements of nearly the same length, and *say what you are going to say, say it, and say you've said it* becomes a recipe for redundancy. The assessment readers' main concern, therefore, was that this writer might be inflexibly wedded to a model that would undermine his responses to assignments in college courses, that he would continue to produce "footstools" when teachers expected more complex and diverse types of "furniture."

The central problem, however, is *not* that the student wrote a five-paragraph essay with three supporting points. Consider this response to the same assessment question, which the readers considered to be the work of a very capable writer:

> *Many factors contribute to an environment where learning occurs. Comfortable settings, skillful teachers, and motivated students all facilitate learning. When all of these factors are positive, something like a chemical reaction happens in the minds of students.*
>
> *Even one negative factor, however, can keep this reaction from happening. Students who have no desire to learn can't be taught, even by the most inspiring teachers. However, even when students are fascinated with the subject, a poor teacher can make learning almost impossible.*
>
> *Unfortunately this happened to me in my senior physics class. Most of us were very interested in science and wanted to go on to college with a strong background in physics. Mr. Gabler failed to satisfy our interests because he spent most of every class period telling us stories about his own experiences that often had nothing to do with science. He seemed to think we needed to be entertained rather than taught, but actually I believe he was the one who was bored with physics and with teaching. I think he was trying to entertain himself.*
>
> *Because Mr. Gabler was such a poor teacher, I had to learn physics mostly on my own by studying the textbook at home. This means that learning can happen without teachers and outside the classroom. If the classroom was uncomfortable or if the other students caused distractions, I could probably learn more by studying alone. If you are motivated to learn something, you can find ways to learn unless some factor makes that "chemistry" impossible.*

> *These examples tell us that missing factors do not hinder learning as much as negative factors do. Although a nice classroom, other good students, and a skillful teacher can all contribute to a good learning environment, learning can happen without them. However, a horrible classroom, disruptive students, and a bad teacher can actually prevent learning.*

This assessment essay is also a five-paragraph theme to the extent that it consists of five paragraphs. Its opening paragraph also introduces three factors that influence a learning environment, and it mentions these factors both in following paragraphs and in the conclusion. Considering these structural similarities, what makes this essay work, in the view of college teachers, whereas the first essay does not?

Unlike the first essay, this discussion of learning uses the three factors listed in the introduction to launch a series of connected paragraphs that lead to an interesting conclusion. In other words, it has a real *beginning, middle,* and *end,* and as a consequence it takes us somewhere, beyond the place where we started out.

We also have a sense that the writer was actually *thinking* about the question both before and while she wrote. She wasn't just dividing the topic into three parts, according to a formula, and filling in the blanks. In fact, I suspect that when she wrote the first paragraph, she wasn't entirely sure where the discussion would end up. The interesting conclusion that "missing factors do not hinder learning as much as negative factors do" may have occurred to her while she was explaining what happened in and outside her physics class. If she had followed the common formula, discussing three separate points in disconnected paragraphs, this idea may not have occurred to her at all.

The basic difference, therefore, is that the second writer used the introductory structure of the five-paragraph model to *initiate* further thought and communication, whereas the first writer used this model to *replace* further thought and communication. The sacrifice of substance for structure can be especially tempting in a timed assessment or essay exam; but the costs of this sacrifice are greater than the first student realized. Experienced teachers could easily recognize his use of a formula to minimize thinking. *The great majority of these teachers want you to use writing as a way of thinking and conveying your thoughts about a subject, not as a demonstration that you can follow a simple recipe.*

What Remains True of Good Writing? _____

If all-purpose formulas for writing are not effective for timed assessments and essay exams, they can completely undermine your ability to complete the more complex and diverse writing assignments we will examine in the next section of this chapter. The freshman I mentioned who always introduced paper topics with a quotation and three subtopics found when she got to college that this format produced acceptable papers in a business class on organizational behavior. In an English class during her second semester, however, the first assignment asked her to address several questions about characters in six short stories. Because her habitual method of structuring essays didn't work for this purpose, she couldn't figure out how to assemble a coherent response. When formulaic models for writing fail or when college teachers tell students to abandon them without offering alternatives, student writers may feel disillusioned and helpless. Meeting the diverse, unpredictable expectations of college teachers can then seem like a hazardous game of chance, as this undergraduate had concluded:

> It's all luck. I used to think I was a good writer, but now I don't know. Sometimes I work for days on a paper, and the teacher hates it. Sometimes I whip it off in a couple of hours, and it turns out great. Maybe it's my mood. Maybe it's the teacher. I don't know. It's always a gamble, so I avoid writing whenever I can, and when I can't avoid it, I just do it, and see what happens.

Writers who were left entirely to their own devices in high school, without models and standards, can face equally difficult problems of adjustment, as this college junior recalled in reference to his AP English class:

> Sometimes I regret having been given so much leeway in writing. It seemed that sometimes I could do no wrong. My writing became more and more embellished. . . . Clichés and pretentious claims were the tricks of my trade. None of my teachers bothered to tell me that half of the time I wasn't even saying anything in my writing. I dealt in trite, pseudo-intellectual discourse when direct, honest answers would have been much more effective.
> College came as something of a shock.

Although the great variety of forms and standards for writing in college defeats the use of a single template, some basic principles of organization and development apply to the great majority of the assignments you will encounter. These principles will not tell you specifically what you should say or how you should structure a particular paper, but in very general terms, they explain how an effective piece of writing typically moves from beginning to end.

Such underlying principles of good writing emphasize movement because writing is, for readers, a linear medium of communication. As the writer, you may revise the introduction of a paper at the end of the process or move passages from one place to another, but a teacher who reads this paper will usually start with the first sentence of the version you turn in and continue reading to the last sentence. *Effective writing, therefore, facilitates continuous reading from beginning to end.*

For this purpose, some underlying principles of the footstool essay hold true—even when its specific features do not—when we include qualities of movement, not just structure. The standard injunction that every essay must have an *introduction, body,* and *conclusion* translates, in terms of movement and the expectations of readers, to a *beginning, middle,* and *end.*

- *Beginnings* are points of departure, when readers expect to learn what this writing is about and the general direction it will take. Even if these beginnings do not explicitly map the routes the writing will travel, they tell us where this journey will start, point us in a certain direction, and provide some bearings for the next move.

- The *middle* portions of an essay (or for that matter of a short story, a report, or a book) should carry the reader smoothly from the point of departure through a series of connected passages. As readers, we shouldn't feel that the route we are taking is completely arbitrary. Even if we do not know *en route* exactly where we will end up, we should feel that that the writer is taking us in a particular direction. We shouldn't feel lost, either in a fog or in a thicket, and if paragraphs can be rearranged without disrupting the flow of the writing, that usually means there is no flow to disrupt. We are just reading a bunch of paragraphs, a random collection of points, disconnected clusters of information.

- You can think of *endings*, then, as destinations. They might or might not present formal conclusions; they might offer new questions, explain what remains unresolved, or point out some new direction for further exploration. But they do give the reader a sense of having arrived somewhere—at some new understanding or a new way of thinking about the topic.

We can condense these qualities of movement into a general definition of good writing in terms of organization and flow:

Good writing establishes a clear point of departure that turns the reader's attention in a particular direction, sustains reading in that direction through a series of connected passages, and leads to a real destination.

This definition of good writing suggests that when you begin to work on an assignment, and while you are writing and revising, you should consider where the writing will start out, the direction in which it will develop, and where it will end up. These factors also explain why it's a good idea to put drafts of your work aside for a while before you revise and edit them. When you read these drafts later with a fresh perspective, you can more easily imagine how they will affect your intended audience—whether readers will be able to follow your explanations, whether your arguments are convincing, and the places where readers will become lost or confused.

Although this general account of the way good writing develops shares some features with standard formats for writing, it does not limit your flexibility in responding to a variety of assignments for readers with different backgrounds and expectations. Here, for example, are the beginnings of two versions of a paper called "What Is Time?," which Paul Shocklee wrote as a freshman in response to an English assignment that asked students to imagine different audiences for writing on a single topic. Shocklee wrote these two versions of his paper for readers who have (in the first version) and do not have (in the second) background knowledge of physics.

Version I

The nature of time has been an essential component of every theory since the beginning of physics. When he wrote down his three axioms of motion, Newton defined time implicitly with the statement "Absolute, true, and mathematical time, of itself, and from its own nature, flows equably without relation to anything external" (Wheeler 40). He set forth this definition so that he could apply his mathematical formalism and not worry that the quantity "t" in his equations might be affected by motion. This Newtonian concept of time as an absolute quantity was taken for granted throughout science, and indeed throughout society, for hundreds of years. However, as sometimes happens in physics, Newton assumed too much when he said that time was absolute.

Near the turn of the century, Einstein showed, in his theory of special relativity, that the concept of absolute time is without meaning, thus completely altering our conception of the nature of time. (39)

Version II

"Does anybody really know what time it is? Does anybody really care?" Chicago's lyrics do not often provoke deep thoughts about the nature of the universe, but in this case, the questions are pretty good. Most people feel familiar with time; it takes sixty seconds to cook minute rice, and classes at Cornell last fifty minutes. What more is there to say?

A lot more, as it turns out. Physicists, the people whose business it is to worry about the things most people take for granted, have been thinking about the problem of time for quite a while. (42)

In the beginnings of the two versions, I included the first paragraph and the transition sentences that lead readers into the middle, or body, of the paper. Both of these versions use the first paragraph to introduce readers to conventional notions of time and then, in following passages, focus attention on alternative theories proposed in physics, with brief explanations of the way time figures in special and general relativity, quantum theory, and current string theory. In both cases, this "destination" underscores the great distance theoretical physics has traveled from Newton's assertion that time is an absolute, unchanging value. But these two versions acknowledge that "points of departure," focus, and forms of explanation will differ for their intended audiences: one accustomed to thinking of time in terms of physics and one accustomed to thinking of time in relation to direct experience.

In the preceding diagram of the five-paragraph theme, we can view the funnel-shaped introduction as an illustration of this introductory task of focusing and directing attention, much in the way that a camera lens brings an object into focus within a broader visual field.

Thinking of the beginning of your paper as a camera lens offers you a more versatile way of dealing with the task of introducing your work to readers. Emphasizing standard parts rather than movement, the formula for the footstool essay tells you that introductions always begin with general statements about the topic and narrow to a list of three points, or a thesis statement. But good introductions do not always consist of these parts in exactly this order. Here are some examples:

- Journalistic writing often begins with a specific *anecdote*, a *quotation*, or some other kind of "hook" to grab the reader's attention.

- Introductions to some academic essays begin or end with a *question* that further passages will try to answer.

- In history and other fields, essays may move chronologically from *one time or event in the past* toward the period, events, or developments the essay will bring into focus.

- Paul Shocklee's essays introduce one *theory* of time as a background for focusing on others as they developed historically.

- An essay about literature or theater may begin with *description* of one scene or character as a point of departure for focusing the reader's attention on a broader theme in the entire work.

As a flexible device, the introduction is a zoom lens that can shift focused attention from a narrow view to a wider one, or the opposite. And these beginnings can extend beyond the first paragraph: through transition sentences in the next paragraph, through the first pages of a long essay, or to the first chapter of a book. Regardless of their length or structure, however, these beginnings should lead readers to a focused awareness of what this writing is about and of the direction it will take toward some destination.

Figuring Out What Assignments Are Asking You to Do

In my tale of the apprentice in the furniture factory, the "departments" I had in mind were obviously academic ones. To give you a sense of the diverse objects that experts in these departments ask apprentice writers to build, we will consider some examples of writing projects assigned in courses primarily for freshmen.

Comparative Literature

An assignment based on the study of Virgil's Aeneid*: Analyze the role that illusion plays in leading such characters as Hector, Anchises, Dido, Turnus, and Aeneas to a misplaced faith in the happy outcomes of events. In a world where human free will rather than Absolute Fate determines the outcome of events, how do ambiguity, misperception, confusion, and misunderstanding complicate the course of human action?*

Film Studies

One of the themes of the film (Citizen Kane*) is Kane's isolation. How do settings, sound, framing, camera angles, and other technical devices emphasize that Kane is cut off from others? Judging from these cues, as well as from the film's narrative elements, would you say that Kane becomes isolated only in old age, or would you say that he is always alone?*

Philosophy

Define "free will" philosophically. In particular, say whether, to act freely, a person doing something must be able to do otherwise. Here you must explain just what the expression "able to do otherwise" means.

Then address two questions: First, is "free will" under your definition compatible with determinism? Second, would Daniel Dennett endorse your definition? Say why you think Dennett would (or would not) endorse your definition of free will.

History

Between the early 1900s and the mid-1930s, American Indian people struggled in several different ways both to participate in the national society of the United States and to preserve their distinctive tribal identities. Evaluate the overall success of this effort.

Political Science

Both Rosencrance ("American Influence in World Politics") and Oye ("International Systems Structure and American Foreign Policy") argue that the structure of the international system creates basic constraints that U.S. policy makers must adjust to. However, Rosencrance's argument rests on a logic of system polarity (the transition from bipolar to multipolar), whereas Oye's argument relies on the logic of declining hegemony.

In a three-page essay, compare and contrast Rosencrance's and Oye's central arguments. What is the logic of each argument? How comparable are each author's assumptions? Do both use the same kinds of evidence? Which of these two views do you find more persuasive? Why?

Business

Read the case study on the declining values of real estate investments held by Woods Development Corporation. Assume that the Board of Directors has decided to cut its losses and, over the past year, has sold 46 percent of this property. Your supervisor in the Accounting Department at Woods has asked you and your two colleagues to draft a 500-word section of the company's annual report to stockholders, explaining this decision and its effects on company earnings, both over the past year and in projections for the future. Your goal is to provide accurate information and analysis that will also reassure investors that these are calculated losses in the long-term interests of a financially healthy corporation.

Biology

The editors of Science *have asked you to write a short piece for one of their boxes describing the process of genetic drift. Your assignment is to describe genetic drift in a way that may be grasped by the unfamiliar reader and used as a background for the other articles in the issue. Strict page limits apply, so your description must not exceed two double-spaced pages.*

Astronomy

Astronomers have big plans to move various ground-based observatories into space (either in orbit or onto the surface of the moon). Choose a proposed space-based observatory, describe why one would want to carry out the work off the earth's surface, and explain what one could hope to accomplish.

Chemistry

For your lab section on March 30, complete a report for your experiment on the "Entropy of a Solution of Potassium Nitrate." Your report should include the usual Abstract, Introduction, Experimental Section, and Results and Discussion according to guidelines in your Lab Manual.

Although these are real assignments—some of them condensed for brevity and comparison from longer versions—we can't entirely put ourselves in the shoes of the students who were taking these classes. In each case, students would approach these tasks with contextual knowledge of the subjects and readings, central objectives of the course, and teachers' expectations. This is why Eduardo, the highly efficient and successful student I described in Chapter 1, viewed every assignment as a separate "puzzle" he had to solve, using information he gathered about the course and teacher.

From these examples, you can also see why I argued that even the best high schools cannot fully prepare their students for college and why a single formula for writing cannot reliably work for all of these purposes. No one, including college professors, can be prepared in advance to perform all these tasks. Even if you studied genetic drift in high school biology or saw the film *Citizen Kane*, you would have difficulty completing the assignments on these topics without understanding the specific circumstances in which the assignments on these topics become meaningful.

Without carefully reading and thinking about the assignments, however, the students taking these courses would not really know what they were doing either. And although we can't entirely solve these puzzles outside the contexts in which they were constructed, important clues reside in the assignments themselves.

The majority of these assignments pose explicit questions for students to answer, or problems they should solve, usually in relation to course readings (or films) and other material. As I've noted, *college teachers use writing assignments primarily to stimulate thought about the subject and to find out what you think.* In most cases, therefore, these assignments explain the questions, problems, or intellectual challenges teachers want you to think through. They will not always explain the forms of writing in which you should organize and present your thoughts, though they usually specify the minimum or maximum length.

To solve the puzzle of an assignment successfully, therefore, you must read the assignment very closely and figure out how to structure an effective response. Apart from the chemistry lab report, which refers students to detailed instructions in a laboratory manual, the Philosophy assignment provides the most obvious guidelines for organization. It tells you to begin with a definition of "free will," with certain conditions specified, and then to answer two questions about the compatibility of that definition: with philosophical determinism and with the views of Daniel Dennett. The form of the assignment itself therefore provides a basic outline for writing:

- Construct a definition of "free will" with stated conditions.
- Address the compatibility of your definition:
    1. with determinism
    2. with the views of Daniel Dennett

The structures of some of the other assignments suggest an organizational framework as well. Following the sequence of questions in the Film Studies assignment on *Citizen Kane*, you would probably begin with analysis of the ways in which "technical devices" in the film create a sense that Kane is isolated. Following an introduction to this central question, you could use the stated list of technical categories ("settings, sound, framing, camera angles, and other technical devices") to sequence paragraphs in this section, although a different order would work just as well in this case. Then you would answer the question about the span of this isolation—whether it characterizes the whole of his life or only the end.

The Business case study assignment also offers a fairly reliable template for writing a brief report to stockholders: (1) explain the company's decision to sell 46 percent of its real estate, (2) explain the short-term and long-term effects of this decision, and (3) provide concluding reassurance that this is a smart decision for a healthy company.

In other cases, however, teachers do not clearly envision or describe the structure of your paper when they are writing the assignment. Considering the intellectual problem they want you to address, they may pose an open question for you to answer, as in the History and Astronomy assignments, or they may present a number of questions and suggestions intended only to stimulate thinking, not to serve as a template for writing. Sometimes there are too many of these listed questions or factors to cover in a single essay, or teachers have presented these ideas in random order as they came to mind. Yet many students will try to use all of these points, in order, as instructions for writing, often with unfortunate results.

The Comparative Literature assignment, for example, asks a general question about "the role that illusion plays in Virgil's *Aeneid*," in making its characters the victims of their own optimism. The assignment lists main characters one might use as examples, and it also lists "ambiguity, misperception, confusion, and misunderstanding" as factors that "complicate the course of human action." In this case, however, the lists provided are just prompts for thinking about the central question, not guidelines for organizing the essay. Following an introductory discussion of the general theme of "misplaced faith" in predetermined fates, you would probably discuss a series of examples from the *Aeneid*, but not necessarily follow the sequence of characters listed in the assignment, and then conclude with a discussion of the patterns you observe among these examples in conflicts between free will and the belief in "Absolute Fate." Trying to discuss the roles of "ambiguity" and other related factors separately, believing that the assignment fated you to do so, would lead you to confusing distractions, making your paper an example of the illusions the assignment asks you to analyze.

As a basis for organization and style, assignments sometimes refer students to models of professional writing in the field. This assignment in Biology asks students to imagine that they are composing an explanation of genetic drift for one of the "boxes" in *Science*. Rather than trying to guess what such writing would be like, clever students will head straight to the library to examine examples of the real item, such as this one, boxed in an article by Dennis Normile in the May 19, 2006, issue of *Science* magazine:

Asian Fusion

Dennis Normile

India, Korea, and possibly Japan are joining China in building next-generation tokamaks. These machines seek to fill a research gap on the road to the International Thermonuclear Experimental Reactor (ITER) by employing all-superconducting coils to study the physics of confining plasmas for long durations, which current tokamaks can't do.

- India's Institute for Plasma Research is now commissioning its Steady State Superconducting Tokamak. An engineering test at cryogenic temperatures turned up problems that are now being addressed. Institute plasma physicist Y. C. Saxena says they are hoping to try a second engineering test later this month. If that goes well, they will attempt their first plasma in the summer. The $45 million project, launched in 1994, is the smallest of the new tokamaks. But Saxena says they believe they can help unravel the physics of long-lasting plasmas.

- The most ambitious machine is the Korean Superconducting Tokamak Reactor (KSTAR) being built by the National Fusion Research Center in Daejeon. KSTAR relies on superconductors made from more advanced niobium-tin alloy that ITER will employ. The $330 million project was delayed because of Korea's late-1990s economic crisis. Project Director Lee Gyung-su says they are now aiming for first plasma in early 2008.

- For several years, Japan's Atomic Energy Agency has been studying the possibility of upgrading its JT-60 tokamak to be fully superconducting. Japan may get funding for the upgrade from the European Union as compensation for its assent to the agreement to build ITER in France. An agency spokesman says key decisions are under negotiation. –D.N.

However thoughtfully they compose their assignments, teachers can't always anticipate the kinds of confusion or misunderstanding their instructions will create. Students who produce the worst papers in the class are typically the ones who fail to ask for clarification when they don't understand what the assignment is asking for. And these failures often result from procrastination. As the deadline approaches, asking a teacher to clarify the assignment will become increasingly awkward and eventually impossible.

As soon as you receive an assignment, therefore, read it carefully and try to envision how you will structure your response. If you can't imagine the type of writing the teacher expects you to produce, ask for clarification as soon as possible.

Structuring Comparisons and Arguments ⎯⎯⎯⎯⎯

Organizational Options for Comparison

The Political Science assignment included in the previous section calls for two types of writing that are frequently used in college classes, especially in the social sciences. This assignment first asks students to *compare* the views of two political theorists, Rosencrance and Oye, and then to *argue* that one or the other is more persuasive. Because these two purposes for writing are so common and are often combined in assignments, we should consider some of the conceptual problems they pose for college students.

Although this assignment indicates two theorists you should compare and lists three factors you should consider, it does not tell you whether you should use the theorists or the factors to organize your comparison. In making this decision, your main goal is to avoid confusion between the two theorists while making points of correspondence and difference clear. If you have to compare two texts (or for that matter two buildings, paintings, or organizations)—A and B—you have two basic choices. One choice is to describe A entirely and then describe B, following a general introduction. If an analysis of the two texts (or the assignment) indicates that they represent a common set of factors—I, II, and III—in each section, you can discuss these factors in the same order. A rough outline in response to the political science assignment would look like this:

Introduction to the texts and issues
A. Rosencrance
    I. Logic
    II. Assumptions
    III. Evidence
B. Oye
    I. Logic
    II. Assumptions
    III. Evidence
Conclusion

The second choice is to use the factors common to the two texts as the main sections of your paper, comparing the two texts in each section in a framework such as this:

Introduction to the texts and issues
I. Logic
    A. Rosencrance
    B. Oye
II. Assumptions
    A. Rosencrance
    B. Oye
III. Evidence
    A. Rosencrance
    B. Oye
Conclusion

Which strategy should you use? In some cases, either would work, and the choice is therefore a matter of preference. As a rule, however, the first approach works best when the paper is fairly short, two or three pages, or when separate accounts of the texts represent them best because they have different features or raise different issues. In a short paper, the reader can keep your full discussion of A in mind as you discuss B. Continually shifting back and forth between A and B will fragment the discussion and make the paper sound choppy.

The second approach usually works best in longer papers and in those that emphasize specific issues more than the whole of the author's perspective. If you spend three or four pages discussing A before you turn your attention to B, the reader may have trouble remembering points of comparison or contrast, especially if there are several.

You can vary these basic schemes in many ways, with different numbers of texts or factors. An assignment might ask you to compare three texts, not two, and you might decide to emphasize two, four, or eight points rather than three. Or you might see one central issue with several implications. One common variant of the second approach begins with *summary introductions* to the texts, then discusses *similarities* (points of correspondence or agreement), then *differences* (points of divergence or conflict), and finally *conclusions*. This strategy can work for short papers or for very long ones.

I should emphasize, however, that *choosing a skeletal framework for organization does not replace thought about the texts and will not in itself produce a fluent, cohesive, interesting paper.* To make an essay work, you must think about the assignment, read the texts carefully, consider the sequence of points you wish to make, establish connections between them, and write fluently within sections.

This thought and effort will be essential because the readings teachers ask you to compare will not tell you what to say about them. Nor are readings likely to correspond as neatly as the idealized outlines sketched previously. Unless authors directly address one another in ongoing arguments, their books and articles rarely parallel each other point for point. It is more likely that teachers will ask you to compare readings that offer different perspectives on related topics. Points of comparison might not be immediately obvious, or there might be only one central point of comparison between readings that are otherwise only marginally related. Writers with different perspectives, furthermore, might *not* disagree.

The Academic Meanings of "Argument"

When teachers ask students to summarize or compare readings and then take a *position* or construct an *argument*, as the Political Science assignment does, students often imagine that assignments such as this ask for their "opinion," and they sometimes begin to respond to the question with the phrase "In my opinion. . . ." The word *opinion* annoys many college teachers (for reasons I'll explain), and I recommend that you delete it from your vocabulary in academic work. To call an idea your "opinion" suggests that it is simply an arbitrary, personal matter of preference that requires no justification and invites no further discussion:

> In my opinion, San Francisco is more interesting than Seattle.
>
> I think *Kill Bill* is a great movie.
>
> Economics is boring.

We often express opinions of this sort in conversation, and most of them pass quietly as matters of individual preference or taste. In the language of argument, such opinions are "uncontested assertions," and as long as they remain uncontested, you don't need to defend them or even to think about them further. Now and then, however, someone will *challenge* these opinions from a different perspective:

> I think Seattle is a fascinating place and much nicer than San Francisco.
>
> *Kill Bill* is just stylish and shallow. In another ten years no one will watch it.
>
> Economics is my favorite course this term, as well as my major.

If you stick with your opinions in the conversations that follow, you will need to support and defend them as *positions*. Now engaged in an argument, or at least in a discussion, you will have to think about your preferences or aversions and explain why you have them. In doing so, you must take the other person's views into account and either refute these views or change your own perspective if you are to reach some kind of understanding.

When teachers ask you to *take a position, present an argument*, or *explain your views*, therefore, they are not just asking for your opinion on the issues at hand. They expect you to engage in a discussion of these issues, acknowledge alternative viewpoints, and explain with reasoning and evidence how you arrived at the position you put forth. Even if teachers disagree with your position, they will appreciate an argument that is thoughtful, well supported, and interesting.

How can you find a position? What makes an argument interesting?

Interesting arguments result from critical reading and thinking, but the meaning of the term *critical* is not the same in academic work as in common usage. When teachers say (as they frequently do) that they want their students to "think and read critically," they do not mean that you should try to find something *wrong* with every reading, every theory, design, or system. They mean that you should think beyond the surface of readings and issues, remain open to alternative perspectives, and, above all, *ask questions*. Thinking and reading critically in college does not mean rushing to judgment and finding fault with every position you encounter, but just the opposite: *suspending judgment, delving into the complexity of issues, examining the way arguments work*, and *considering questions that remain unanswered*.

For this purpose, the adage "There are two sides to every argument" is false. There are many sides to every argument, and the most interesting ones will result from the questions you ask about the most obvious, polar positions in a debate:

Should we limit greenhouse gas emissions that cause global warming?

If you leap too quickly, uncritically, to the "yes" or "no" side of this debate, you will miss the complex issues it raises, and your argument will not be very interesting. If you pause to ask further questions, your perspectives will become increasingly deep and rich—open to positions that reflect the intricate problems this central question poses:

- What evidence indicates that global warming is actually occurring?
- Do we know whether this warming is progressive or cyclical?
- Do gas emissions cause this phenomenon?
- Which gases cause it?
- How and where are these gases produced?
- How can they be limited, and at what costs?
- What levels of emission are acceptable?

- Who should establish and enforce these limits?
- What further information do we need?

The kinds of arguments or positions that result from critical thinking in academic work rarely coincide with popular meanings of the word *argument*, such as "verbal attack" or "shouting match." Even when scholars are personally, passionately invested in their positions, academic arguments usually take the form and style of rational, dispassionate discussion, their *assertions* (statements that something is true) supported by evidence and logical explanation rather than invective.

Due to this emphasis on logic and evidence in all academic discourse (both writing and speaking), it can be difficult to distinguish efforts to *persuade* the audience, through argument, from attempts to *explain, describe, interpret,* or *solve.* In a popular college writing text called *Everything's an Argument*, the authors take the position that "all language—including the language of visual images or of symbol systems other than writing—is persuasive, pointing in a direction and asking for a response." From this perspective, even when you try to describe something "objectively," you are asking your audience to look at the object in a particular way. Even when you present explanations based on "factual" information, you are persuading the audience to accept your choice and use of evidence. Although arguments can be explicit or implicit to varying degrees, your responsibilities in constructing good arguments and for constructing good summaries, explanations, or comparisons are not fundamentally different. Many types of writing, such as the Political Science assignment we examined, also combine these forms and purposes for writing.

The emphasis on logic and evidence in academic writing does not mean that you should avoid all uses of the first person ("I" or "we") or that your writing must be extremely formal, impersonal, and "dry" to be credible. Some assignments will ask you to link course material to your own experience, and scholars often use the first person to refer to their own research or perspectives. This student used the first person to distinguish her own views on genetic testing and health insurance, supported by logic and evidence, in a paragraph that captures an appropriate style of argument in academic writing:

> *The current system of using risk management seems outdated given the technological advances that have occurred since its implementation.*

What began as a method of using actual previous claims to determine appropriate premiums (Kass, 1992) has turned into a mess of complicated predictions. Consider also that most genetic disorders cannot be detected through testing; does it seem fair that some people should pay more just because their genetic risk is detectable while others of potential risk pay low rates? As Kevin Goddard of the Vermont Blue Cross said, "Insurance is assuming risk, spreading risk, and managing risk" (Murray, 1992). Since not all risks can be equally determined for the purpose of setting premiums, I suggest a return to community rating as a way to spread and manage risk.

The Form and Flow of a Scientific Report _____

Perhaps a footstool essay, of sorts, remains a reliable formula for one particular type of college writing. Yet the occasions for using this model in science labs are so remote from the high school English class, where such formulas for writing usually originate, that college students rarely notice the similarities.

Among the examples of writing assignments listed in this chapter, only the Chemistry lab report calls for the use of a standard format, including the "usual" sequence of sections: Abstract, Introduction, Experimental Section, and Results and Discussion. This assignment also refers students to "guidelines in your Lab Manual," which provides detailed instructions for completing these sections of a scientific report, including a sample report and guidelines for presenting tables, graphs, and equations. Oddly enough, you will probably receive the most elaborate, explicit instructions for writing not in your English class or in other humanities courses but in the laboratory components of your science courses. And although the divisions among report sections and specific instructions for completing them may differ from one science class to another, the basic form of a scientific report remains fairly consistent. Following an *Abstract* (a brief summary of the entire report), information will be organized in this typical sequence:

Introduction

Methods (sometimes called the *Experimental* section or *Materials and Methods*)

Results

Discussion/Conclusions (sometimes combined with *Results*)

The predictable form of a scientific report makes writing one seem deceptively simple and very different from the essays assigned in many other courses. Undergraduates have told me that lab reports at first seemed a mysterious, alien form of writing and gradually became a routine task of putting information in the right places, according to a prescribed format described in their laboratory manuals. They often conclude that scientific writing isn't *really* writing at all—only a matter of "getting the facts straight," making sure that introductory facts are somewhere in the introduction, methodological facts are in the methods section, and so on.

But scientific reports *are* real forms of writing, more widely used and important in academic work than you may realize in your first years of college when they seem to be isolated formulas for presenting information in science labs. As we will see, principles of structure and movement that accommodate the expectations of readers in other types of writing apply to the scientific report as well. In this form, as in others, good writing will not result from filling in the blanks of a prescribed format.

The Form of a Scientific Report

When I asked a group of chemistry graduate students to describe the shape of a typical experimental report, they settled on the shape of a martini glass, because the methods and results sections are very specific

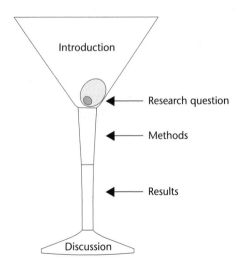

in comparison with the introduction and conclusion. The introduction moves from the general subject or principles of the research to the specific research question or hypothesis (represented by the olive in their diagram), which lands at the bottom of the introduction.

You can easily see the resemblance of this diagram to that of the five-paragraph theme or keyhole essay presented at the beginning of this chapter. In both cases, the funnel-shaped introduction moves from the general topic to the specific research question or hypothesis, which corresponds with the position of the "thesis statement" in many essay formulas. A description of the specific methods and then the results of the experiment (or field study) comprise the middle sections or "body" of the report, which leads readers to the broader discussion of these results and their significance.

Narrative Flow through Categorical Sections

Features of many introductory science courses encourage students to think of the lab report as a series of buckets for different types of information or as a test of their ability to follow instructions. In an introductory laboratory, you probably won't be doing original research. In fact, you may be doing the same experiment that everyone else in the class is doing, following detailed procedures in a lab manual to learn well-known principles and methods, toward predictable results. In addition, science lab courses often use grading methods that assign points for the accuracy and placement of individual pieces of information, not for the organization and clarity of the writer's explanations.

Such grading schemes and "cookbook" experiments might lead you to believe that the organization and flow of writing within the sections will not matter. In practice, however, disorganized, poorly written reports typically receive low grades, even if they include most of the necessary information. In her research on "Students and Professionals Writing Biology: Disciplinary Work and Apprentice Storytellers," Sharon Stockton found that the standards biology teachers use to grade lab reports often differ from the standards described in course guidelines. As the title of Stockton's study suggests, scientific reports are not just containers for facts; they are also "stories" about the experiment, and *teachers evaluate the way those stories are told, even if they seem only to be scanning for points.*

If you think of the scientific report as a particular kind of story, the challenge of writing one effectively will seem less mysterious and more directly related to other kinds of writing you do. Although scientific research has become increasingly specialized and its language increasingly technical, scientists have been telling essentially the same kinds of stories about their research for more than 200 years. Early scientific reports were first-person narratives, often published as "letters" describing particular discoveries the authors made in the laboratory, on expeditions, or through simple observation.

By the end of the eighteenth century, frequent challenges to their claims had forced authors to *explain their intentions, describe the experiments* in ways that could be tested, and *substantiate the results*. With or without formal headings, the sections of a report fell into a consistent order, which is still used in professional articles and student reports. You can think of the sections of a scientific report as answers to a logical series of questions about your experiment:

Introduction: What were you doing and why?

Methods: How did you do it?

Results: What did you find out?

Discussion: What do the results mean?

Most reports also begin with an *abstract*, which is a brief summary of the entire project, including a sentence or two each about the research problem, the experimental methods, the major findings, and their importance. Although the abstract appears at the beginning of the report, authors usually write it last, when the rest is finished.

Scientists tell these stories about investigation in a certain order because changing the order wouldn't make sense. Good storytellers would not explain the meaning of results before they had presented these results, they would not describe the results of an experiment before they described that experiment, and they would not describe those methods before they explained what they were doing and why.

On behalf of your readers, therefore, the basic principles of movement that produce good writing for other kinds of assignments apply to scientific reports as well. **A good report will establish a point of departure from which it focuses the reader's attention in a particular direction, and it will sustain reading in that direction toward a destination.**

The Broader Uses of Scientific Narration

These principles of organization and flow will apply to all of the scientific writing you do, regardless of variations in specific guidelines or among the preferences of individual teachers. They will also apply to much of the assigned reading you will do, especially in advanced courses. The narrative structure I described, as answers to a series of questions, is the predominant model for describing research in all of the sciences and social sciences and even in some branches of the humanities. When your teachers publish articles based on their own research, the great majority of them will use some version of this model. Even if they do not use formal headings for the sequence of sections, they will, in a predictable order, introduce their research topic and questions, describe their methods, report the results of their research, and conclude with a discussion of what these results mean in their fields of study.

Students in the first two years of college often assume that the uses of scientific reports are confined to science classes only because they rarely do firsthand research in other fields of study. When you read "primary" research articles in the sciences and social sciences, however, you will recognize this pervasive narrative form. And if you do original social or scientific research projects in fields such as sociology, anthropology, psychology, or business, answering this sequence of questions—*What were you doing and why? How did you do it? What did you find out? What do these results mean?*—will provide a natural framework for describing your research.

Variations and Preferences

Although the basic form and flow of a research report remains fairly consistent among different courses and fields of study, this form has many variations. Some of the differences in formats, styles, and documentation systems represent standards for research reports in particular fields, described in style manuals such as that of the American Chemical Society (ACS) or the American Psychological Association (APA). Other variations represent the preferences of individual teachers in relation to the purposes of writing in their courses. As I noted, science courses usually provide detailed instructions for completing reports, and you should read and follow these instructions carefully.

In the sciences, as in other fields, individual teachers also have unstated preferences that influence their evaluations of student writing and other features of presentations, so you should assume that the standards for presentation are high. Like many other kinds of literature, the stories scientists tell about their research are usually illustrated, and in some cases these tables and figures—graphs, drawings, photographs—are extremely important parts of the text. For every student who underestimates the importance of organization and flow in a lab report, another will underestimate the importance of clear, accurate figures.

When grading exercises with chemistry teachers, for example, I found that evaluation of tables and figures was the greatest cause of variation when several teachers were grading the same report. Some teachers are not very concerned about the appearance of a graph or chart as long as it contains the necessary information. Others become extremely annoyed when figures are sloppily drawn, poorly labeled, or difficult to read. These differing standards often amounted to as much as a full letter grade on the report. Yet most of these teachers had not conveyed their preferences to students because they *assumed* everyone shared their views.

Because you can't predict which kind of teacher you will get, it makes sense to put thought and care into graphs, charts, and tables. These illustrations should be centered at logical places in relation to the text, with numbers (*Figure 1* or *Table 3*) and accurate labels. On graphs, axes should be labeled as well, with clear lines and data points. The bars in bar graphs should also be clearly distinguished with labels and shading or color. Most undergraduates have access to software for drawing figures and tabulating data in highly legible forms. If you do not, draw figures and tables neatly on graph paper and trace them onto the text pages of your report with a good black pen, and type the labels.

What individual teachers will like or dislike isn't entirely predictable, but all teachers like to read sentences and passages that flow smoothly, have a logical sequence, and vary in length and form. If you keep in mind that a scientific report is a story that must be told well, *listen* to the way your report sounds, and revise any sentences or paragraphs that sound awkward. Your report will be much clearer and easier to read. Teachers who have to evaluate twenty or thirty of these reports will be grateful for your efforts!

A Brief Summary

Although some features of organization and movement apply to almost all of the writing you do in college, a survey of actual assignments across the curriculum reveals a great variety of specific forms, purposes, and standards that differ widely even within a field of study. In other words, there are no reliable formulas for *all* writing in college, nor can you reliably predict what a history teacher or a biology teacher will ask you to do in an assignment. Even scientific reports—the most uniform of all types of academic writing—can vary considerably according to specific teachers' goals and preferences. **The main challenge you will face, therefore, is doing what particular assignments and teachers are asking you to do within the larger context of a specific course.**

I emphasize the obvious because undergraduates so often do *not* do what the assignment asked them to do but something they thought they should do, something they were once taught to do, or something they always do when writing essays.

Because assignments will not tell you exactly what you should write, responding to them effectively is not a simple or slavish matter of following instructions. Good assignments provide a structure—a set of constraints—within which you can write freely, demonstrating your knowledge, creative intelligence, and skill. If you misinterpret that structure of expectations, you will not know where your freedom lies. If you spend five or ten minutes just reading and thinking about an assignment, registering what it asks you to do, and trying to imagine the kind of paper that would meet those expectations, you can use that freedom with a stronger, more accurate sense of composure.

GUIDELINES

- A large proportion of college students have learned to use an all-purpose formula for organizing essays, such as the "five-paragraph theme," which I've compared with learning carpentry only by building footstools (p. 108). In college, however, teachers expect you to use your writing skills to produce "furniture" of many kinds, including summaries, comparisons, arguments, and reports.

- For these diverse purposes, you must replace all-purpose formats with a general concept of good writing that embraces variation and emphasizes *thought,* *connections,* and *movement* from a beginning, through the middle, to the end. In these terms, good writing establishes a clear point of departure that turns the reader's attention in a particular direction, sustains reading in that direction through a series of connected passages, and leads to a real destination (pp. 114–18).

- When applying these general principles to specific assignments, your first challenge is figuring out exactly what particular assignments and teachers are asking you to do within the larger contexts of their courses (pp. 118–24).

- Although students tend to think of scientific reports as distinct types of writing for reporting facts in categorical sections, good scientific reports conform to my general definition of "good" writing. Scientific reports are essentially narratives—stories about the research—that answer a logical series of questions, which are explained on pp. 132–33.

- With or without formal headings and sections, this narrative order applies to most research-based writing in the social sciences and some branches of the humanities as well. You can use this organizational framework for some research papers and for understanding assigned readings that report on research.

7 | Writing in Reference to Others

> Human communication is never one way. Always, it not only calls for response but is shaped in its very form and content by anticipated response.
>
> This is not to say that I am sure how the other will respond to what I say. But I have to be able to conjecture a possible range of responses at least in some vague way. I have to be somehow in the mind of the other in advance in order to enter with my message, and he or she must be inside my mind.
>
> —Walter Ong, *Orality and Literacy*

A Bubble of Solitude, Abuzz with Conversation

Compared to speaking, writing usually feels like a solitary experience. To maintain concentration, most writers prefer to work alone, behind closed doors in their homes or offices. As a college student, you may write in public places, such as libraries or cafés, but even in those settings writing occurs—in your mind and on paper or on a computer screen—in a little bubble of solitude. As a writer, you are thinking and saying things unrelated to your surroundings, in a voice no one around you can hear. As the poet William Stafford observed, this is what makes writing, in contrast with speaking, "one of the great, free human activities": the fact that you are completely free to say anything in writing without immediate consequences. While considering the writing process in Chapter 4, we noted that writing becomes an act of communication only when you choose to *release* your work to readers. Until that point of release, while you are writing in this private domain of thought and expression, no one can judge or contradict what you are saying.

I may seem to be contradicting myself, then, when I say that most academic writing is also *discursive*: part of a discussion, conversation, or argument with others. While you are writing, you may be alone and are free to say anything. Potential readers are not there, are not yet reading, and remain in some ways hypothetical. But you enjoy this freedom only because the participants in written conversations are dislocated in time and space. The great power of writing includes the freedom to converse with readers in the future and, as a reader yourself, with other writers in the past, including those who are no longer alive. In their own writing, produced recently or long ago, the captured voices and ideas of these authors remain accessible to you, specific, and real, as your writing will be for those who read and respond to it in the future.

These discursive dimensions of writing become especially important in academic work, because research in every field builds on or departs from related studies in the past and influences studies in the future. A research question that one scholar tries to answer emerges from findings and arguments among other scholars, and this new addition to an ongoing discussion will stimulate further research and debate. "My own field," one biochemist told me, "is a beehive of communication"—one that includes many kinds of written and spoken exchanges. The romantic notion of a brilliant scientist making startling discoveries alone is almost entirely a fiction. In some fields, works of literature, philosophy, history, or science in the past become the primary objects of investigation, requiring frequent quotation, summary, and other references to these texts, along with references to the work of other scholars who have studied them. In the narrative form of a research article, which we discussed in Chapter 6, answers to the question "What were you doing and why?" include explanations of what other scholars did and said as well. The freedom that writing offers to us—to assemble conversations with others across time and space— therefore carries responsibility for making these references to others clear and accurate.

In the great majority of their writing assignments, college teachers hope to engage you in these discussions with other authors or with other kinds of "texts," such as films, speeches, or works of art. When assignments ask you to "discuss" an issue or "present an argument" in reference to course readings, therefore, you face the challenge of distinguishing the participants in this conversation—clearly establishing your own voice and position as the writer, and addressing the reader, in relation to the words and ideas of other writers.

Like the principles of organization and movement discussed in Chapter 6, clear references to others serve one underlying purpose: *to keep the reader from getting confused.* And in ways I'll explain, basic strategies for clarifying these references rely on a combination of common sense and language skills that you already possess. For student writers, however, the added necessity of *documenting* sources, with complex and unfamiliar reference systems, often undermines these skills and sensibilities. "Academic discourse" can then seem an alien form of writing—a web of rules, obligations, and potential errors fundamentally different both from the freedom and privacy of self-expression and from the natural flow of conversation.

Formal systems for citing and documenting sources are indeed complicated sets of rules and conventions that (to make matters worse) differ among the various fields of study. When you are writing a paper with multiple sources of information, your responsibility to use the correct citation format may distract you from the more basic, familiar challenge of making sure the reader knows who is saying what. But don't let these details of formatting throw you off balance as a writer. In a later section, I'll explain how and why academic writers use these documentation systems. Here I'll just mention that these systems help readers to identify and locate the sources of quotations and other references in your writing. Correct documentation, therefore, is a matter of following instructions and imitating examples, for purposes largely separate from the more familiar and important goal of maintaining clarity in your writing.

The Familiar Principles of Referring to Others _____

When you as a writer distinguish *your* language and ideas from those of others, the methods of reference in academic writing are not very different from the methods used in popular writing, such as journalism, or in casual written or spoken exchanges.

Whenever you tell a story that involves other people, you have to distinguish their parts in the story: what *they* said and did and when. In conversation, you will make these distinctions more or less naturally. Communicating directly with a particular audience, you will automatically establish your own voice as the narrator because listeners can see and hear you speaking, you can see them listening, and they can reply. In this narrative voice, you then distinguish the voices and actions of others with phrases like "Then Kevin said . . ." or "When I saw her the next day, Cheryl explained that. . . ."

For clarity in writing, you have to make the same kinds of distinctions, establishing your own presence, voice, and viewpoint as the writer, addressing an imagined audience in reference to other writers or speakers in some kind of chronological or logical sequence. And the basic challenges of distinguishing all of these voices and references are essentially the same in all kinds of writing. In written communication, in contrast with speech, your own voice and presence are not visible or so obviously distinguished, so you have to make these distinctions clear in the way you write. For this purpose, however, you have some special, visible tools in writing, such as quotation marks.

Even the most informal written exchanges often require the use of these tools and distinctions to clarify references to several other people and sources of information. Imagine, for example, that you are writing an e-mail message to a friend from home, Ellen, who attends another school. Suppose that in this message you convey the news you've received about a recent, serious argument between two other mutual friends, Tony and Carol. In this message to Ellen, you explain that you first learned about this conflict in a message from Tony. You summarize Tony's version of events and quote part of his message. Then you tell Ellen about a later phone conversation with Carol and explain what she said happened. You conclude your message by explaining to Ellen why you think Tony's story is more credible and why Carol is being unreasonable.

Making sure that Ellen understands who said what, when, and how, as well as what you think about the situation requires fairly complicated writing skills, but they are also routine, well-practiced operations for any of us who indulge in e-mail gossip. In your communication with Ellen, for example, you wouldn't just drop a quotation from Tony's message into your own without introducing it with a "tag" such as "At the end of his message, Tony said. . . ." And if you included a large part of his message, you would probably paste it in as a separate block. Are these methods fundamentally different from the reference-management skills you need for writing academic essays based on published writing? Not really. To observe the similarities, reconsider the Political Science assignment discussed in Chapter 6:

> *Both Rosencrance (American Influence in World Politics) and Oye (International Systems Structure and American Foreign Policy) argue that the structure of the international system creates basic constraints that U.S. policy makers must adjust to. However, Rosencrance's argument rests on a logic of system polarity (the transition from bipolar to multipolar), whereas Oye's argument relies on the logic of declining hegemony.*
>
> *In a three-page essay, compare and contrast Rosencrance's and Oye's central arguments. What is the logic of each argument? How comparable are each author's assumptions? Do both use the same kinds of evidence? Which of these two views do you find more persuasive? Why?*

In this paper, as in the hypothetical e-mail message, you should explain two sides of an argument and present your own views on the issue. To make these positions and references clear, you must establish your own voice as the writer who is addressing an audience, presumably your teacher. With that voice and with that audience in mind, you need to distinguish and summarize what Rosencrance and Oye had to say about constraints on U.S. policy makers, with reference to the sources of their ideas. When it becomes useful, you will probably include direct quotations from these authors and will need to introduce these quotations to indicate who is "speaking" in your work, with phrases such as "At the beginning of *American Influence in World Politics*, Rosencrance explains . . ." (or says, observes, notes, argues, concedes, contends, asks, or any number of other verbs) to indicate the specific nature of the quotation and avoid repetition.

Again, these goals, distinctions, and methods apply to all kinds of writing that involve references to others both in and outside academic work. In college writing, they apply equally to short papers that refer to one text and to long research papers that use many sources. And these principles for distinguishing voices, language, and ideas in your writing hold true whether you are or are not citing and documenting sources as well. *Formal documentation systems have their own purposes that do not replace your responsibility for clearly indicating who is saying what.*

In most magazines and newspapers, authors maintain responsibility for distinguishing the words and ideas of others without using formal citations or bibliographies. For example, in an article titled "Green Manhattan" (published in the October 18, 2004, issue of *The New Yorker*), David Owen argues that although "most Americans, including most New Yorkers, think of New York City as an ecological nightmare, . . . it's a model of environmental responsibility." In building this argument, Owen uses many kinds of references and quotations, including conversations, interviews, historical documents, and academic publications. Although his article does not document these sources with formal citations, page numbers, or a bibliography, Owen always clearly introduces them to the reader, distinguishing their voices and ideas from his own. Here is an example of a quote from a conversation:

> *"Anyplace that has such tall buildings and heavy traffic is obviously an environmental disaster—except that it isn't," John Holtzclaw, a transportation consultant for the Sierra Club and the National Resources Defense Council, told me.*

Owen uses essentially the same method for introducing published sources. Having mentioned recent books in his office, he writes:

> *At the top of the pile is* Out of Gas: The End of the Age of Oil, *by David Goodstein, a professor at the California Institute of Technology, which was published earlier this year. "The world will soon start to run out of conventionally produced, cheap oil," Goodstein begins.*

In his own voice, referring directly to the author, Owen then summarizes Goodstein's argument in one long sentence, with a direct quotation from Goodstein spliced onto the end:

> *In succeeding pages, he lucidly explains that humans have consumed almost a trillion barrels of oil (that's forty-two trillion gallons), or about half of the earth's total supply; that a devastating global petroleum crisis will begin not when we have pumped the last barrel out of the ground but when we have reached the halfway point, because at the moment, for the first time in history, the line representing supply will fall through the line representing demand; that we will probably pass that point in the following decade, if we haven't passed it already; that various*

well-established laws of economics are about to assert themselves, with disastrous repercussions for almost everything; and that "civilization as we know it will come to an end unless we can find a way to live without fossil fuels."

In Owen's article, as in other examples of good journalism, while we are reading we always know who is saying what, and often when and where as well, without having to look for the reference in a footnote or bibliography. These responsibilities for distinguishing voices and introducing references apply equally to student writers and scholars. The additional use of parenthetical citations, footnotes or endnotes, and bibliographies in academic writing simply makes it easier for readers to locate these references. If you wanted to find Owen's last quotation from Goodstein's book, for example, you would have no page number to help you. In another part of his article, Owen quotes Thomas Jefferson's statement that cities are "pestilential to the morals, the health, and the liberties of man" but does not tell us the source of Jefferson's statement. Because readers of academic publications are often engaged in their own studies of the same or related subjects, they may need exact titles, names of publishers, dates of publication, page numbers, and other information to find referenced sources.

Providing the specific information about references that audiences need to understand and evaluate what you are saying serves the basic principle of *clarity*. But doing so is also a matter of *honesty* and *courtesy*. In the example of the imaginary e-mail message, unless you wanted to mislead Ellen, you would try to give her accurate, honest accounts of what Tony and Carol previously told you about their sides of the argument, distinguishing quotations and summaries of what they said from your own interpretations and conclusions. You would try to be fair to Tony, to Carol (your *references* or *sources*), and also to Ellen (your *audience* or *reader*).

Why are these introductory references also a matter of courtesy? If a friend of yours joined a conversation with people you knew but your friend did not, I trust that you would introduce your friend to the other people present. And you would probably do this immediately so the other people wouldn't have to wonder, "Who is this?" for very long. Your responsibility to make introductions, as the only person present who knows everyone, is a courtesy both to your friend and to other members of the conversation.

The same principles of clarity, honesty, and courtesy apply to references in academic writing. To help your readers to understand who is saying what (and perhaps also when and where), you need to use your own voice as the writer to introduce sources to the reader, clearly distinguish their voices and ideas from yours, and represent what they have said as accurately and fairly as possible. When you shift between their words and ideas to your own, the reader should have no difficulty making these distinctions.

Misconceptions of Reference and Documentation

If common sense and experience tell us how to follow these basic principles in conversation and informal writing, why do students have so much trouble handling references effectively in formal writing assignments?

I noted that the complexity of academic documentation systems and confusion about their purposes often undermine the basic goal of making references clear to the reader. Student writers often believe that the use of correct citations replaces responsibility for introducing and distinguishing references in the texts of their work. Such misconceptions or false rules commonly reduce the clarity, accuracy, and overall quality of student papers based on references to other work. These misunderstandings can create the appearances, at least, of dishonesty: forms of plagiarism and other violations of academic integrity codes. I'll discuss three of these misconceptions.

That a citation at the end of a paragraph authorizes all uses of that source in previous sentences. To observe how this false assumption undermines the basic principles of reference, consider the following paragraph from a research paper on HIV/AIDS:

> *Exactly how HIV overwhelms the immune system is a concept that is not exactly understood. Several major hypotheses of disease progression state that HIV pathogenicity is a direct result of virus adaptation to the host environment. The evolution of new viral phenotypes that invade the host's immune responses is believed to play a major role in disease progression. Studies need to investigate the role of viral evolution in disease progression by following genetic divergence and diversity over the course*

of infection while differentiating between adaptive and selectively neutral changes. Quantifying the rate and pattern of adaptive evolution within infected patients is crucial to understanding the development of AIDS. (Williamson, 2003)

In this passage, and throughout her paper, the writer assumed that a parenthetical citation at the end of a paragraph allowed her to use that reference freely throughout the paragraph without distinguishing her views and language from those of the cited source. But in what parts of the paragraph, exactly, is this writer addressing us in her own voice from her own perspective, and where is she quoting Williamson? Does the citation refer only to the last sentence or to the entire paragraph? Is it the writer's belief, for example, that "studies need to investigate the role of viral evolution in disease progression," or is she simply paraphrasing Williamson's recommendation? We cannot answer these questions without locating and reading the Williamson article and comparing his statements with the writer's, and readers should not have to do this additional work to understand who is saying what.

In fact, almost everything in that paragraph was either paraphrased or quoted verbatim from the source cited at the end. And although this writer was not trying to deceive anyone, her use of sentences and phrases from the source without quotation violates codes of academic integrity at every college or university. The belief that a citation legitimizes any use of that reference is therefore not only false but hazardous.

That minor changes in wording allow you to use an author's language and ideas without reference, quotation, or citation.   When student writers find ideas and information in readings that are useful for their own writing, they often mistakenly believe that they can appropriate that material as their own by making a few changes to the original. But this is comparable to convincing yourself that a stolen car is yours because you changed the paint and hubcaps. With similar logic, writers sometimes assume that they can "borrow" exact phrases or even sentences from a source without quotation if these statements represent their own beliefs—what they "really wanted to say." These temptations may result from the effort to avoid continuous quotations and citations when you feel that everything you have to say comes from your sources or from the effort to write a paper directly from your research notes (problems I'll help to resolve in Chapter 8).

To illustrate what I mean, here is a passage on robotics from Steven a Pinker's book *The Language Instinct*:

> *But household robots are still confined to science fiction. The main lesson of thirty-five years of AI [Artificial Intelligence] research is that the hard problems are easy and the easy problems are hard. The mental abilities of a four-year-old that we take for granted—recognizing a face, lifting a pencil, walking across a room, answering a question—in fact solve some of the hardest engineering problems ever conceived (192–93).*

And here is an uncomfortably close paraphrase of the same passage that, when passed off as the writer's own work, drifts into plagiarism:

> *The helpful household robots of science fiction have not become a reality. Over thirty-five years of research, the field of Artificial Intelligence has demonstrated that the hard problems are easy to solve and the easy problems are hard. A four-year-old can easily recognize a face, walk across a room, pick up objects, and answer simple questions, but these are some of the hardest problems AI engineers have tried to solve.*

Like other experienced teachers, I can usually "hear" these patchworks of voices running through individual passages and whole papers, creating the impression that no one in particular is the author. When I convey my suspicions, the writers usually admit that they were writing directly from sources and had trouble avoiding close, continual paraphrasing.

If you find yourself deliberately changing words and phrases or rearranging information from a source for the purpose of passing it off as your own writing, that intention itself should tell you that you are indebted to the source and must acknowledge and cite the reference, distinguishing paraphrasing from quotation. Otherwise you will be misusing the source and violating principles of academic integrity. In the following section on Integrating References, I'll discuss strategies for avoiding these pitfalls, but here is an example of one clear, correct way to refer to the passage from Pinker's book in your own writing:

> *In* The Language Instinct, *Steven Pinker explains why robots have not become common household appliances, in spite of predictions in computer science and science fiction. These predictions failed to materialize, he says, because in the field of Artificial Intelligence, even the most basic mental and physical skills of children, such as walking, turned out to be "some of the hardest engineering problems ever conceived" (192–93).*

Because this paragraph begins with voiced reference to the source, the reader knows it is a paraphrase of information in Pinker's book and can distinguish the exact quotation, at the end, from the summary of his ideas.

That quotations do not need an introduction to the reference if you include a citation at the end.   This misconception results from the more general, false assumption that citation and documentation replace the need to make references clear in the text of your work, as journalists do. And this belief results in what writing teachers and editors call "dropped quotations" or what I sometimes describe as "mysterious voices." The quotation marks tell readers that they have encountered the voice of someone other than the author of this paper. But whose voice is it exactly? Here is one example of a dropped quotation from a paper written for a sociology class:

> Like their colleagues in anthropology, sociologists who lived in the communities they studied had to redefine their roles as observers and their relations with the subjects of their research. "My relationship with Doc changed rapidly in this early Cornerville period. At first he was simply a key informant—and also my sponsor. As we spent more time together, I ceased to treat him as a passive informant. I discussed with him quite frankly what I was trying to do, what problems were puzzling me, and so on. Much of our time was spent in this discussion of ideas and observations, so that Doc became, in a very real sense, a collaborator in the research" (Whyte, 1943, p. 300). These collaborative relations characterized research methods known as "participant observation."

The sudden appearance of this long quotation seems especially mysterious because it is a first-person account of a personal relationship, yet we have no idea who is "speaking" to us. The author no doubt assumed that the citation for Whyte at the end of the quotation answered this question and perhaps also that readers in sociology would know that this citation referred to William F. Whyte's classic example of participant observation, his book *Street Corner Society*.

To understand and evaluate a quotation, however, readers usually need to know its source when they begin to read it, not after. They should not have to skip ahead to the parenthetical citation (or, for footnote or endnote systems, to the bottom of the page or to the end of the text) to figure out who said this. In most cases, furthermore, they won't be able to identify the source from the author's last name in the citation, and they should not have to turn to the Works Cited page to figure it out. A simple introduction to the source and context—for example, "In *Street Corner Society*, published in 1943, William F. Whyte gave us an early description of these collaborative roles"—would solve these problems.

Although dropped quotations are not forms of dishonesty, they do undermine principles of clarity and courtesy in the use of references. This practice is so common in student writing that teachers usually try to ignore it as a minor annoyance, often because they can't explain the solutions or don't have time to do so. If you learn to introduce quotations and other references clearly, however, your writing will be considerably easier for teachers to read and closer to professional standards for academic writing.

Integrating References: The Importance of Voice

All of these misconceptions about the use of references in academic writing, along with some forms of plagiarism, are also problems in the use of voice. At the beginning of this chapter, I emphasized the fundamental importance of establishing your own voice as a writer in relation to others. Doing this effectively even has my vote for *the most important set of skills student writers can develop*—skills that most reliably distinguish accomplished writers from novices. If your own voice isn't working to address and direct the reader, you can't clearly indicate, summarize, interpret, quote, or evaluate what other writers said. Without a voice of your own for these purposes, you can't really participate in academic discussions.

Earlier in the chapter, for example, we saw a paragraph from a research paper on HIV/AIDS. When I talked with the writer about her difficulties in handling references in her work, she quickly revealed her misconception that a citation "covered" all uses of the reference in that paragraph, but she didn't know what else she could do when she was writing about "what other writers said." When an assignment asked her to explain her own views or to describe her own experiences, she could establish her own voice as the writer without difficulty—without even trying to do so. But explaining what she learned from readings, she said, was a completely different kind of writing. "What happens to your voice then?" I asked. "Oh, it vanishes!" she replied immediately.

What is this "voice," exactly, that she lost and needed to restore? In reference to the distinctive style or tone of an author's writing, voice is a difficult, subtle quality to define. And this is what students often *think* I mean when I tell them that they should write about subjects and readings in their own voices. They believe they should write in a recognizably "personal style" or use first person pronouns to state their own opinions.

But that isn't what I mean. In casual communication, as I've noted, you establish your voice naturally, automatically, when you address the reader directly and distinguish what you are saying from what others have said. In academic writing, you establish your voice just as easily when you introduce references to the reader. If the writer of the research paper on HIV/AIDS, for example, had immediately introduced the Williamson article to the reader as the main source of information in that paragraph, she could have continued to use that reference with clarity and honesty:

> *In his 2003 study of "Adaptation in the env gene of HIV-1 and Evolutionary Theories of Disease Progression," Scott Williamson acknowledges that "The exact mechanisms by which HIV overwhelms the immune system remain poorly understood" (p. 1318).*

Having introduced her source, she could use an exact quotation and avoid the extremely close paraphrase at the beginning of her paragraph. Then she could continue to summarize or quote from Williamson's article without appropriating his voice and drifting into plagiarism.

Using your voice as the writer to introduce and integrate sources, you take charge of your writing and responsibility for it, as all students and scholars must. This kind of writing isn't just about "what other writers said" but about what *you* choose to tell us about the subject, including the words and ideas of other authors you choose to include. When you take this responsibility for telling your own story about the subject, you gain tremendous freedom to use the work of other writers to help you tell this story well.

When you have introduced sources to the reader, you can explain, or summarize, what these authors said in your own words, or you can let them "speak" directly to the reader through quotation. As long as you use quotation marks around the language you have included from references, you can splice borrowed words, phrases, whole sentences, or passages into your own writing for your own purposes. Suppose, for example, that you are writing a paper on population control policies and want to refer to this passage from Joel Cohen's book *How Many People Can the Earth Support?*:

> *My first discovery was that I was not alone in not knowing how many people the Earth could support. Numerical estimates produced over the past century have ranged widely—so widely that they could not all be close to right—from less than 1 billion to more than 1,000 billion. More than half of the estimates fell between 4 billion and 16 billion people.*
>
> *I also learned that the question "How many people can the Earth support?" is not a question like "How old are you?" which has exactly one answer at any given time. The Earth's capacity to support people is determined partly by processes that the human and natural sciences have yet to understand, and partly by choices that we and our descendents have yet to make (10–11).*

You might want to include the entire passage in a block quotation, as I just did, but there are many ways to use portions of Cohen's writing in your own. You might begin, for example, by summarizing the central purpose of his book and then quoting portions that underscore the main points you want to convey:

> *In* How Many People Can the Earth Support?, *Joel Cohen explains that all efforts to calculate sustainable population growth depend on diverse assumptions and variables that yield radically different answers to the question posed in the title of his book. As a result of these variables, Cohen notes, "Numerical estimates produced over the past century have ranged widely—so widely that they could not all be close to right—from less than 1 billion to more than 1,000 billion." Because sustainability will depend on "processes that the human and natural sciences have yet to understand" and on "choices that we and our descendents have yet to make," Cohen recognizes that this central question raises hundreds of others, some of which we cannot yet answer (10–11).*

Note that you can splice whole sentences onto your own or quote parts of sentences within yours. In the first sentence quoted above, the capital N and the period tell the reader that you have quoted the entire sentence without alteration. In the next sentence, lowercase initial letters and the absence of end punctuation indicate that you have quoted portions of sentences. When you first introduce a reference, include the author's full name. After that, you can use just the last name for references. "Tags," such as "Cohen notes" or "recognizes," remind the reader of the source and sometimes express the author's viewpoint.

If necessary, however, you can leave out language within a quotation or add language to it, as long as you indicate to the reader that you have done so. You can indicate missing language with an *ellipsis* (. . .) and added language with square brackets ([ ]). For example, if you do not want to include the phrase between dashes (*so widely that they could not all be close to right*), you can insert an ellipsis to let the reader know you have dropped it:

> *As a result of these variables, Cohen notes, "Numerical estimates produced over the past century have ranged widely . . . from less than 1 billion to more than 1,000 billion" (10).*

If you cut off the end of a sentence so it will appear complete, you should let the reader know you have done so by using an ellipsis and a period at the end:

> *As a result of these variables, Cohen notes, "Numerical estimates produced over the past century have ranged widely . . . ." (10).*

Brackets allow you to supply information that clarifies a quotation or makes it fit grammatically with your sentence. When you take sentences out of a longer passage, for example, you might need to add words that clarify pronouns:

> *"Apparently they [Pearl and Reed] did not at first know that Verhulst had derived the same curve . . ." (85).*

Or you might need to substitute words that allow the quotation to mesh with your sentence:

> *Cohen's "first discovery was that [he] was not alone . . ." (10).*

Only three rules limit your freedom to integrate quotations within your own sentences and passages:

1. The readers should always know whose language they are reading.
2. Sentences you assemble with quotations should read grammatically.
3. Your use of quotation (including splices, ellipses, and brackets) should not distort the original meaning of the quoted material.

These methods of integrating quotations and references will require more experimental tinkering than just dropping quotations, as mysterious voices, into the middle of your work. With practice, however, weaving references and quotations into your own writing will also become a natural way to compose.

Why and How We Use Documentation Systems ____

I've emphasized these methods of establishing voice and integrating references because college students so often lose their voices and their control over writing when they mistakenly believe that formal citations make references clear. If anything, the opposite is true. In journalism and other kinds of popular writing, we observe that writers can clearly distinguish voices and indicate sources of information *without* using formal citations or bibliographies. In fact, lots of parenthetical citations or distracting footnotes in academic writing can interfere with the flow of a text for the reader. But this observation raises another question: *If writers can make references clear to readers without formal documentation, why do college teachers ask you to include citations and bibliographies in your writing?*

Although documentation systems aren't necessary for distinguishing sources, they are very useful for locating, checking, and comparing sources in further research and discussion. Even in popular articles, books, and web documents, authors provide full references (titles, dates of publication, publishers, page numbers, or web locations) if they want to make sure that you can find sources. This specific information is more consistently useful in academic writing.

The detailed systems of documentation you must use in many writing assignments therefore originate in those scholarly "beehives of communication" that your professors inhabit, in lively communication with other scholars in their fields. While general readers are usually content to read about a subject, other experts on that subject are more likely to want to find a referenced source, use that information in their own research, verify cited claims, or check the meaning of a quotation by reading it in context. To pursue these further inquiries easily, they need full references and page numbers.

Why doesn't everyone use the same system? Like many other inconsistencies among components with similar functions, such as computer or auto parts, differences among documentation formats result from independent development. Documentation formats and other details of presentation developed as guidelines for publication in specific professional organizations and publications, such as the MLA (Modern Language Association), the APA (American Psychological Association), and the ACS (American Chemical Society). Each of these organizations has a main professional journal with guidelines for the formats of submitted manuscripts, and each also publishes a more detailed "style guide" used for publications (and student papers) in its own and related fields.

Each of these systems offers the benefits of familiar, consistent, standardized formats for writers, publishers, and readers *within* an area of research who do not need to shift from one system to another. The disadvantages of these variations fall almost exclusively on student writers, who complete papers in a number of fields and may have to use two or three different documentation systems in a single term. Inconsistencies then seem pointlessly confusing, especially when they are minor, arbitrary details of punctuation or sequence in a Works Cited entry. But some of these variations reflect real differences among the goals, forms, and subjects of writing in particular fields.

When should you use a documentation format? Some writing assignments, such as the one on the *Aeneid* in Comparative Literature, (p. 119) will ask you to discuss features of a single text, which you would logically introduce at the beginning of your paper. Unless you also refer to published studies of that text or to other work by that author, you don't need to document that single source to constantly remind the reader that your reference is "in the *Aeneid*" or to point out that "as Virgil wrote. . . ." When you are referring to or quoting passages in a book, however, you should note the page number in parentheses after the reference or in a footnote in case your reader wants to find the passage.

If your paper involves two or more texts, as in the political science assignment on Rosencrance and Oye (pp. 119–20), the same principles will probably apply. You can introduce the references in the text of your paper, distinguish references to the authors in your own writing, and include page numbers when you quote particular parts of their work. If these are assigned readings, you probably do not need to list the sources at the end, although some teachers may ask you to do so. *If you are using additional sources, however, you should cite references and list them at the end of your paper.*

If you are using more than two sources of information (including electronic sources), you should certainly use a documentation system, including citations in the text or endnotes and a Works Cited page. Remember that the choices you make in these matters are on behalf of your readers out of consideration for the information they might need.

Which format should you use?   In their assignments, on a course syllabus, or in class, teachers often specify the documentation system they want you to use in their courses. If they do not, don't hesitate to ask. In some cases, they may tell you they don't care which system you use, as long as you follow it consistently.

As a rule of thumb, however, you can expect that teachers in branches of the humanities (such as English, comparative literature, or philosophy) will prefer that you use the MLA system, if only because it is familiar to them. Teachers in the social sciences (such as psychology, sociology, or anthropology) will probably prefer that you use the APA system. Teachers in various branches of historical studies often prefer the CMS (*Chicago Manual of Style*) system, which places the numerous citations in these studies in footnotes or endnotes where they will not interrupt the flow of the writing.

Teachers in the sciences and in fields such as business are less predictable. Individual sciences, mathematics, and business have style guides for their own publications, and teachers sometimes request that you use these formats for writing in the forms of typical publications, such as scientific or business reports or research proposals. One reason is that guidelines in these fields include detailed instructions for presenting graphs, tables, equations, and technical information that are specific to that field of inquiry. When teachers in these subjects assign more general essays on readings or issues, however, they may accept any consistent format or even prefer the APA or MLA systems. Teachers in some branches of business (such as organizational behavior), for example, consider themselves to be social scientists and often use the APA system.

To give you a sense for the basic differences between systems, we'll take a brief look at the three formats used most commonly for writing assignments in college. To use these and other formats consistently, however, you will need more detailed guidelines and examples.

MLA Format

In the MLA system, if you have introduced the source with the author's name in the text, you can cite the reference at the end of the quotation or paraphrase by simply including the page number in parentheses:

> In an open letter to Ezra Pound that follows the introduction to A Vision, Yeats offered the immodest prediction that his book would "when finished, proclaim a new divinity" (27).

If you have not introduced the author by name in the text, include the author's last name before the page number in the parentheses: (Yeats 27). If your paper includes references to more than one publication by an author and you do not introduce the specific title, you should include a brief title in the parentheses: (Vision 27).

All of these parenthetical citations in the text refer your readers to the bibliography and should, when combined with names or titles in the text of your paper, allow the reader to find that source easily in your list of Works Cited. Here is the basic form of a bibliographical entry in the MLA format:

> Yeats, William Butler. A Vision. New York: Collier Books, 1969.

APA Format

The APA system accomplishes the same task of referring readers to the bibliography with a combination of the author's last name and the date of publication. If you have introduced the author in the text, place the publication year in parentheses immediately after the name:

> Bruno Latour and Steve Woolgar (1986) described the motivations of scientists to publish in economic terms, as "cycles of credit," measured in terms of "investment and return" (p. 190).

In this system, page numbers are used primarily after direct quotations, often in separate parentheses from the date of publication. If you have not introduced the authors' names in the text, you should include their last names and the publication date in parentheses, separated by a comma:

> In interviews about their motivations to publish, scientists often use economic terms such as "credit" or "investment and return" (Latour & Woolgar, 1986).

Reference to the publication date refers the reader to bibliographical entries that are somewhat different from the MLA form. Notice that the APA bibliography usually lists only the initials of the authors' first names, followed by the date of publication:

> Latour, B., & Woolgar, S. (1986). *Laboratory life: The construction of scientific facts.* Princeton: Princeton University Press.

CMS Format

Both the MLA and APA formats interrupt the visual flow of the text with parenthetical citations, within or at the ends of sentences. To reduce this distraction, writers in fields such as history (in which the narrative flow of the writing is especially important) often prefer to use the CMS format, which removes citations to the bottom of the page (as footnotes) or to the end of the text (as endnotes). These notes are numbered sequentially throughout the paper and are indicated by superscripts at the ends of quotations and other references.

For example, in her paper on the "Genealogy of the Third Reich: The Connection between Nietzschean and Nazi Ideas," written for a German Studies seminar, Anastasia Poushkareva included this reference in CMS format:

> What might have spurred the nationalist feelings of the Nazis is Nietzsche's profound dissection of etymology, which establishes "the distinguishing word for nobility, finally the good for the good, noble, pure, originally meant the blond-headed, in contradistinction to the dark, black-haired aboriginal inhabitants."[3]

In the "Notes" at the end of the paper, the reader can find the source of this reference in the numbered sequence and the page number for the quotation:

3. Friedrich Nietzsche, "Genealogy of Morals." In *Basic Writings of Nietzsche*. Ed. Walter Kaufmann (New York: The Modern Library, 2000), 466.

If the next reference refers to the same text, you can note this with the simple abbreviation "Ibid.," followed by the page number for that citation:

4. Ibid., 473.

The Bibliography or Works Cited page lists this reference by the author's last name, in alphabetical order, with page numbers for the entire essay within the text:

Nietzsche, Friedrich. "Genealogy of Morals." In *Basic Writings of Nietzsche*. Ed. Walter Kaufmann. New York: The Modern Library, 2000, 460–92.

At this point, I should mention that footnotes and endnotes have a purpose in addition to citation: providing further information or comments from the author that are secondary or marginal to the text. These supplementary notes can be used in MLA, APA, or CMS formats, where they are included, in numbered sequence, with the citations.

Where can you find these formats?   I know students who construct citations and bibliographies on an ad hoc basis each time they write a paper by imitating the examples in assigned readings for that course. This will usually get the job done, for better or worse. But finding the right examples this way is inefficient and sometimes difficult if you must list an unusual type of reference, such as an essay in an edited collection or a unique electronic source. It will be far more convenient to use a single, detailed reference for the appropriate system. These are the three main sources for this information:

- **A college-level handbook of grammar and composition.** You may already have one of these from a writing course. These handbooks usually include condensed versions of the MLA and APA documentation systems, with sample citations and Works Cited entries of different types and, in some cases, examples of research papers.

The most comprehensive handbooks may include descriptions of the CMS system and others. The concise guidelines and examples they provide are usually sufficient for handling references correctly in college assignments such as research papers. One of these hand-books, either in print or electronic form, will be a useful reference for many kinds of information about grammar, punctuation, and other standards for college work. All college students should own one, and they are always available at campus bookstores.

- **A style guide for the type of writing you are doing.** When you choose a major and write primarily in one area of the curriculum, you may want to purchase the appropriate style guide. These are the published guides for the three main documentation systems used in college work:

  APA: American Psychological Association. *Publication Manual of the American Psychological Association*, 5th ed. Washington, D.C.: APA, 2001.

  CMS: *The Chicago Manual of Style*, 15th ed. Chicago: University of Chicago Press, 2003.

  MLA: Gibaldi, Joseph. *MLA Handbook for Writers of Research Papers*, 6th ed. New York: MLA, 2003.

- **Campus libraries and writing centers.** These are useful resources for information and assistance in conducting research and using documentation systems. Reference sections of libraries contain copies of the handbooks and style guides listed above, and most writing centers have collections of these references as well. Most college and university libraries and many writing centers also have guidelines for documentation and style available on their Web sites. If those at your school do not, you can easily locate other electronic guidelines through a browser search for the system you want to use, such as "APA Documentation."

How and When to Cite Electronic Sources

Whenever you use information, ideas, or quotations from electronic sources, you should cite and fully document those references as you would for other publications. So much published material has now been posted on the Internet or made available through electronic databases, in fact, that the distinctions between electronic and printed, published sources are no longer very clear. Web browsers and search engines give you direct access to vast amounts of published and unpublished information. Some periodicals, many individual articles, and other useful materials are published only in electronic forms. Other periodicals or articles appear both in printed and electronic versions. Even the term *library research* now refers to work you can often do on your computer, with access to electronic catalogues and their links to databases of published material that you can often download and print directly.

With further variations among formats, types of electronic sources have expanded beyond my ability to provide detailed descriptions in this brief text. For the same reasons, you can't expect to remember all of these details for documenting various types of electronic sources with different systems. For this purpose, you should consult *recent* guidelines in a style manual or handbook for writers or current information posted on documentation Web sites. As the types and combinations of resources proliferate, editors of style manuals and handbooks have had to develop new guidelines, and older editions may not include examples of electronic sources you now use. Here I'll simply point out some basic patterns and pitfalls.

In popular writing and in casual communication, writers often refer readers to Web sites simply by their web address, or URL (uniform resource locator). *For this reason, and some others, student writers often imagine that a cryptic URL is sufficient documentation for an electronic source, but it is not.* This practice is comparable to listing only the Library of Congress call number for a published source. You would not expect readers to go to the library catalogue to figure out where you got published information, so you shouldn't expect them to use a web browser to identify your electronic sources. The relevant information for properly documenting electronic sources may differ from those for printed sources, but the basic principles of clarity, honesty, and courtesy remain the same.

For a Works Cited list, full documentation of a Web site may include *the name of the author, the title of the site, the names of editors (if any), the date the site was created or last updated, the sponsor of the site (if different from the author), the date on which you used the source, and the URL*. The order in which this information should appear depends on the format.

For example, here are Works Cited entries in MLA, APA, and CMS formats for a very useful Web site: the home page for the Online Writing Lab (OWL) Web site at Purdue University. This Web site includes many sections on writing, research, and documentation, with links to other useful sites and resources.

MLA

Driscoll, Dana Lynn. The OWL at Purdue. 20 Sept. 2006. Online
 Writing Lab (OWL), Purdue University. 4 Jan. 2007. <http://
 www.owl.english.purdue.edu/owl/>.

APA

Driscoll, Dana Lynn (2006, September 20). *The OWL at Purdue.*
 Retrieved January 3, 2007, from Online Writing Lab (OWL)
 Web site, Purdue University: http://www.owl.english.purdue
 .edu/owl/.

CMS

Driscoll, Dana Lynn. *The OWL at Purdue.* http://www.owl.english
 .purdue.edu/owl/. 20 September 2006.

You will notice that the order and formatting of these entries differ in the three systems, and the kinds of information that Web sites provide also differ considerably. While published books and articles will always provide standard information in predictable locations, Web sites may not list authors or dates of postings or revisions. This information can also be difficult to find on web pages, which authors are free to design without following conventions. In documenting sites, however, you *must* provide all of the relevant information you can locate, and in the APA system, if the site's creation date is unavailable, you should indicate this by placing (n.d.) in parentheses.

Many other specific conventions apply to documentation of other types of electronic sources, such as electronic periodicals, articles retrieved from database services, portions of books published online, postings on e-mail or web discussions, and visual material. As I've noted, following all of these detailed guidelines requires access to recently revised formats offered in writing handbooks, style guides, or library and writing center Web sites.

When you use formats that cite textual references in parentheses, such as MLA and APA, *citations* of electronic sources do not differ substantially from those for published work. In these systems, brief references to the author or title, date of publication, or page numbers refer readers to the Works Cited list, where they will find full documentation. In formats such as CMS that use footnote or endnote citations, however, the distinctive documentation forms used for electronic sources apply to citations as well, because the first noted reference to a source, electronic or not, must include full documentation. *In footnotes or endnotes, as in Works Cited entries, a URL is not a sufficient form of citation.*

Because the forms of electronic sources and the formats for documenting them are so complex, it's especially important for you to record relevant information about your sources as you use them. Searching the Internet for a source you forgot to document can be just as time-consuming as returning to the library to check the page numbers or publication date of an article. At the very least, remember to bookmark and clearly label sites you plan to use, and you can save even more time by writing down the necessary information for documentation in your notes or on printed copies from sources.

GUIDELINES

- Think of academic writing as part of a discussion or conversation with others.

- In this discussion, immediately establish your own voice as the writer, addressing the reader in reference to other sources of information and ideas.

- Remember that the main purpose of reference, in writing as in conversation, is *clarity*: to make sure the audience always knows *who* says *what*, and often *when* and *where* as well (pp. 140–45).

- Remember that formal documentation and citations do not in themselves make references clear to the reader; they simply add information about sources.

- For purposes of documentation, use one system or format (such as MLA or APA) consistently, consulting guidelines for correctly documenting specific kinds of references (pp. 155–58).

- For efficiency and accuracy, record bibliographical information for documenting sources, including page numbers, in your notes while you are using references.

- In reference to electronic sources, follow the same principles of clarity, honesty, and courtesy that apply to publications, along with consistency in following the guidelines for a particular format (pp. 159–62).

8 | Research Papers

> Successive drafts of my own talk did not lead to a clearer vision because it simply was not my vision. I, like so many of my students, was reproducing acceptable truths, imitating the gestures and rituals of the academy, not having confidence enough in my own ideas, nor trusting the native language I had learned. I had surrendered my own authority to someone else, to those other authorial voices.
>
> — Nancy Sommers, "Between the Drafts"

What Is a Research Paper?

The principles of reference and documentation explained in Chapter 7 apply to any assignment that requires multiple sources of information, regardless of its length or purpose. Whether a paper is two or twenty pages long, devoted to a summary of readings or to making a convincing argument on an issue, you must address the reader in your own voice and clearly distinguish your language and ideas from those of other writers.

In these respects, the large-scale assignments called *research papers* (or sometimes *term papers* when they are due at the end of a term) do not represent a distinct category of student writing. The research papers assigned in college do not require any consistent form, style, or purpose that distinguishes them from shorter papers in the same fields of study. In these long papers, as in shorter ones, teachers may expect you to *explain* what you have learned about a subject; to *pose and answer a question*; to *take a position* on an issue; to *interpret* texts or events; to *compare* different theories; or to *report* on lab experiments, field studies, or statistical analyses. Teachers sometimes list choices of specific research topics for you to investigate, or they may expect you to choose a topic on your own. The lengths of assigned research papers also vary considerably, from as few as six or eight pages to thirty pages or more. Here are some examples:

- A professor in a literature course asks you to compare central themes in the work of two American poets.

- A professor in political science asks you to analyze the main interests at stake in a recent international conflict and propose terms for a negotiated settlement.

- A professor in ecology asks you to develop an inventory of plant species at a specific study site.

All three of these teachers might call their assignments "research papers," but they would require very different research methods, types of references, and forms of writing. Each of these projects would also differ, I suspect, from research papers you wrote in high school.

Considering these and other variations, what do college teachers mean when they announce that their courses will include a research paper? What, if anything, do these diverse assignments and types of writing have in common?

The most common features of research papers result not from their forms or content but from the general reasons for which teachers assign these projects, their length and importance in a course, and the time required to complete them. When teachers include research papers in their courses, you can reasonably assume that (1) the teacher assigned this work to give you a taste of real investigation in that field; (2) you will have to complete this work in stages over a period of several weeks; (3) you will have to locate, use, and document several sources of information; and (4) this work will count for a substantial portion of your course grade, usually from 30 to 60 percent.

In high school and in preparation for college work, you may have written similarly lengthy, investigative papers that required several references and the use of a formal documentation system. These were probably called research papers as well, and the four features just listed often lead students to the false conclusion that this term represents both a *type* of academic writing and a *way* of writing—a standard set of procedures that are appropriate for every class in high school or college. The length and complexity of these assignments and the time required to complete them do pose some consistent challenges for student writers. In college studies, however, research subjects, methods, and related forms of writing vary so radically that there is no single, reliable method for meeting these challenges effectively. For research papers, as for other, shorter writing assignments, methods you used successfully in high school will not necessarily work in college. Effective strategies for completing a research paper in one college course, furthermore, will not necessarily work for research papers in other courses and fields of study.

For a large proportion of college students, these challenges of completing very different research projects in a single term are quite real. In high schools, research papers are usually assigned in English classes or occasionally in subjects such as history or social studies. In colleges and universities, teachers assign research papers in a much wider variety of courses, and in one semester or quarter, students often need to complete two or three of these important projects in different areas of study. All of these assignments will require specific kinds of research and writing for distinct purposes. And because the final versions of research papers are typically due at the end of a term, in the midst of other assignments and impending final exams, you will need to plan carefully to distribute work on these projects over preceding weeks. In this kind of writing, procrastination becomes especially hazardous.

What really distinguishes research papers from other types of college writing, therefore, are the time-management skills and methods required for successfully completing these large-scale projects. Any of the three examples of research topics listed at the beginning of this section could be assigned as a four-page paper. Assigned as longer research papers, however, the same topics would require more extensive investigation, deeper analysis, and the use of additional references, completed through intermittent periods of planning, research, drafting, and revision.

The Standard Method (and Why It Rarely Works)

To understand how routine methods for completing research papers can undermine the quality of your work, we should first discuss why college professors so frequently assign these projects, often in courses that require no other forms of graded writing.

The most general reason is that research is central to the professions of college teachers and to the production of knowledge in their fields. When professors simply want you to learn *what* experts in their fields already know, they can deliver that knowledge most efficiently through lectures and assigned readings, using examinations to measure how much of that knowledge you absorbed. In addition, however, most college teachers want you to understand *how* scholars *identify significant questions, pursue lines of inquiry, address unresolved issues, support their arguments with evidence,* and *communicate their findings.* These kinds of learning require active participation in discussion and investigation. Research projects offer one way of engaging you in the real work of scholars and members of other professions that require research, in areas such as law, business, health care, social services, and engineering.

When they take the trouble to assign and read research papers, therefore, these scholars are not just interested in making sure that you have located relevant information on a topic. Instead, college teachers almost invariably describe research projects in their courses as *intellectual* exercises that engage you in analytical, interpretive, or critical *thinking* about research material. They hope you will share some of their own curiosity and fascination with this kind of investigation, along with the satisfaction they get from sharing the results of their research with others. As readers, they also hope to encounter new ideas, if only in the way *you* assemble your own understanding of the subject. Most of these teachers will be disappointed, therefore, if you simply repackage information you found, without identifying and pursuing a significant question from your own perspective.

Too often, students miss this intellectual point of a research project and approach it instead as an academic treasure hunt, treating the research paper as a record of the material they found or as a report on the contents of their research notes. As one physics professor observed, "They just want to tell you what the territory looked like as they passed over it."

This common tendency explains why teachers who have a great variety of specific goals for research projects describe fairly consistent weaknesses among the research papers they read:

- The topic is too broad and unfocused.
- The writer doesn't pose a real question, take a real position, or write with a sense of purpose.
- The body of the paper consists of clumps of information from sources, roughly sorted into categories.

- Sources are inappropriate or out of date.

- The writer doesn't clearly distinguish her voice and viewpoint from those of cited authors, or she depends too heavily on these sources.

- The paper seems disorganized, with the most promising ideas buried in body paragraphs or presented only in the conclusion.

These weaknesses result not only from the general misconception that a research paper is a compilation of research notes but also from specific methods students use for research and writing. I can describe these typical methods as a series of instructions:

1. Choose a topic.

2. Locate sources of information on the topic.

3. Read through this material, taking notes and recording useful quotations.

4. Construct an outline from the categories of information you have gathered.

5. Following your outline and notes, write the sections of the paper, incorporating source material in appropriate sections.

6. Complete citations and add a bibliography (or Works Cited list).

7. Check the paper over for errors and typos, and turn it in.

Like the one-draft method for completing shorter assignments, this may appear to be the most logical, efficient way to get the job done. All of its components are necessary, and when writing teachers and others schedule work on research papers, these are often the stages at which they want to check on your progress. What could be wrong with this approach?

These procedures are not so much wrong as insufficient, because they leave out the process of inquiry through which students find a sense of *authority* and become *authors*: writers who have something in particular to say. In themselves, therefore, these methods describe a meaningless exercise. You could use them to complete a paper without ever finding real interest in the subject, without raising or answering a question of your own, and without developing your own thoughts about the issues and information you include. As I'll explain in the last section of this chapter, these steps could be used as a recipe for plagiarism, in which the "writing" in Step 5 is simply assembling the work of other writers. And because you can follow them without developing your own voice and viewpoint as a writer, these procedures can make plagiarism difficult to avoid.

Above all, however, this routine assembly of references is a lost opportunity. If you think of it as a real investigation based on your own interest, a research project can become the most rewarding learning experience you will have in college. I still vividly recall some of the research papers I completed as an undergraduate, even when I've forgotten almost everything else about the courses in which they were assigned. These projects stand out in my memory because I was not just reporting what the "real" authorities said. Through the process of research and writing, I *became* an authority on very specific subjects and developed strong motivations for communicating my ideas. When professors assign research papers, this is the kind of learning experience they hope you will have.

Revising and Adapting Your Strategies

While these are lofty, admirable goals, professors often underestimate the difficulty of finding a position of authority for writing about significant questions in their fields of research. They forget that for scholars like themselves, research questions emerge from a broad *frame of reference* based on years of study that includes previous research and debate exchanged in professional conferences and publications. How can undergraduates like you, who have just begun to study the subject, figure out what is important or interesting? How can you bring a research question into focus within a broader frame of reference?

To some extent, the course itself will provide this frame of reference. In a course called "International Environmental Issues," for example, lectures and readings build the foundations for understanding key environmental problems and recognizing the "actors" (such as government agencies, nongovernmental organizations, and interest groups) most involved. With this background, students can identify a particular case they would like to investigate more deeply, analyze the roles and investments of relevant actors, and make policy recommendations. For the limited purpose of writing that paper, they can potentially build a frame of reference that is sufficient to bring a specific case or issue into focus from their own perspectives, against a conceptual background presented in the introduction. In his effort to make sure topics are in focus within frames of reference, this professor requires a brief proposal and list of references early in the process, and he also comments on rough drafts before the final deadline.

Even with this background and guidance, however, students in the course often turn in unfocused papers that simply rehash a loose assortment of references. And when I talk with students about the causes of these problems, I usually find that for convenience or through habit they followed the Standard Method described in the previous section, without establishing the frame of reference, voice, and perspective that such assignments require. Because all of the components of this method are in some ways necessary, teachers have difficulty explaining what students should do differently. For this reason, I'll discuss the stages of this Standard Method in order, explaining what is missing or inappropriate for college-level work and presenting alternative strategies. And for reasons that will become obvious, problems and alternatives at one stage will affect others as well.

Choose a Topic

The problem.   You will get into trouble from the very beginning of the process if you imagine that "choosing a topic" completes the task of deciding what the paper will be about. Unless your teacher assigns a focused research question, the topic you choose at this point will simply represent a category of information you intend to explore — a point of departure for your investigation, *not* for the paper you will eventually write. In other words, you might confuse an initial *research topic* with a *research question, thesis,* or *position.*

This is why professors so often complain that research papers are too broad and unfocused. The writers have simply chosen a topic, gathered information on that topic, and written the paper from that information without locating a focused question or viewpoint in the process. At best, then, the paper will look like a good encyclopedia entry. For reasons that will become apparent at the next stage, most of the topics students initially choose embody hundreds if not thousands of potential research questions. Over many years of teaching and collaboration with other teachers, I can't recall a single student research paper topic that was too narrow.

Solutions.   When you have chosen a topic for research, constantly remind yourself that this is only a point of departure in the process of identifying a real question or developing a real viewpoint from which you can write. This process should continue throughout your research and even into the phase of writing a first draft. The whole process of research and writing should be one of figuring out specifically what *you* want to say about a specific question.

For example, an American history professor once complained that a student in her class had written a research paper on the topic "Slavery in South Carolina." For a student who knew very little about the subject, this was a reasonable point of departure. While gathering information, however, he had not continued to narrow the topic or to ask further questions. In response to the paper, therefore, his professor *did* ask questions:

What about slavery in South Carolina?

Why are you writing this paper?

Why should I want to read it?

In the process of reading general information on this subject, the student should have begun immediately to look for a narrower topic and for specific questions to pursue.

What does this mean in practice? Imagine that while you were investigating the general topic of slavery in South Carolina, you learned that *the city of Charleston was the main port for the slave trade to the Americas in the eighteenth century, due in part to the need for slaves in the large rice and indigo plantations along the coast.* If you were using the Standard Method, this discovery would simply represent one piece of information among many that you would try to include in a patched-together summary of your research notes on the topic.

For the purpose of narrowing and focusing your research, instead, thinking further *about* this information would raise many specific questions. Each of these questions, in turn, would suggest a particular line of inquiry for an interesting, focused research paper. When you chose to answer one of these questions, that choice would also focus your research strategies and sources of information:

How did the development of rice farming along the coast affect the slave trade into the port of Charleston?

This question would lead you to investigate the methods of rice farming on large plantations along the coastal estuaries of the Carolinas. In the process, you would understand why this agriculture was so labor-intensive and difficult and why it created a growing demand for African slaves in preference over American Indians. In addition to background information on the growth of the slave trade in Charleston, you would look for firsthand accounts and secondary studies of the rice plantations, including descriptions of the farming practices and the lives of slaves on these estates.

> How were slaves distributed from Charleston, as the port of entry, to other regions of the South?

In answering this question, you might first investigate the history of Charleston, focusing on the slave market and the systems through which slaves were sold to new owners. Slave narratives and historical studies of the system would also give you insights into the experiences of "human chattel" in being sold as property, separated from other members of their families, and transported to unfamiliar places.

> How and how frequently did slaves escape from owners in this region?

This question would focus your research primarily on the published narratives of escaped slaves and on secondary studies about these narratives, along with histories of the Fugitive Slave Act and its effects on efforts to assist or recapture those seeking freedom from slavery.

Embedded in this one corner of "Slavery in South Carolina" are dozens of other interesting research questions as well:

> How did the slave trade affect the economy of Charleston?
>
> What were the roles and living conditions of urban slaves?
>
> What were the differences between coastal and inland agriculture, and how did these differences affect living and working conditions for slaves in these areas?

Each of these questions would send you down a somewhat different path of inquiry from the others. If the assignment called for an argument, through the process of research you would need not only to identify a question but to develop a position on the issue. You won't be able to do this at the beginning when you know little about the subject, so the task of refining your topic and developing a position must continue throughout your research.

Because this process requires further thought, changing strategies, and investigation of new sources, students often imagine that it will be more difficult than just choosing a broad topic and, in the next step, finding one bunch of sources. Early refinement and focus actually make the processes of research and writing much easier, especially in the later stages. And apart from the higher quality of the results, trying to answer an intriguing question is much more enjoyable than just gathering and piecing together a lot of information.

Locate Sources of Information on the Topic

The problem.   The methods of topic selection and research that are taught in high schools are often based on the small scales of school and public libraries, where a subject index may locate only a few sources. Students can then locate all of the available references at once, in a separate stage, before they begin to read about the topic. Because college library systems may contain more than 3 million books and subscribe to thousands of periodicals, a subject search on a broad topic will locate too much material, most of it outdated or inappropriate in other ways. If you try to use high school search methods in a large library, you can spend many hours sifting through references to find the few that are useful. Even if you have narrowed your topic, subject searches will turn up many sources you won't want to use and will exclude some of the best material on a topic. One reason for this is that subject listings include work that is devoted primarily to that topic, whereas the best sources might be on related subjects that are listed under different headings. As a consequence, this strategy will rarely lead you directly to the information you need.

In the Cornell online catalogue, for example, a search for books under "slavery" produced 5,000 titles listed by subheadings. The great majority of these books were on slavery in America, with about forty of them under the subheading "South Carolina." These forty books, however, are not necessarily the best sources on the subject. Most of the three or four thousand titles on slavery in America contain extensive references to South Carolina, and thousands of other books and articles on related topics (such as the political and social history of the South) might be useful.

Internet searches can be even more random, inefficient approaches that turn up huge numbers of useless references and miss most of the useful ones. A general Google search on "slavery in South Carolina," for example, listed more than 5 million sites that contained references to these words. Even if you enjoy browsing, you can't afford to spend hours sorting through this material, nor can you afford to use references uncritically — a problem that is especially serious on the Internet, where screening systems are unreliable.

Remember that you are writing a research paper for scholars who are concerned about the quality of information used to support arguments and explanations. Ideas and information are not necessarily valid just because they appeared in print or on a Web site. Biased and outdated sources can seriously undermine the quality of your paper, even if your own ideas are sound.

Solutions.   *First, aim for quality rather than quantity, and use good references to find others.* This advice applies equally to library and Internet research methods, which have become increasingly interwoven. Regardless of your research question, it's not a good idea to try to gather all of your source material at once, before you begin to study the subject. If you can find one authoritative, recent reference in the debris of a subject search, stop browsing and turn immediately to this source. Good books, scholarly articles, and many Internet sites have bibliographies of related material, usually of similar quality. Use these bibliographies as search tools, locating the most promising titles they list. The literature cited in a good reference will also contain bibliographies, and these chains of reference will efficiently locate materials of consistent quality and focus that are already related as pieces of a "conversation" among scholars. When you search for material in the library, ask for help from the reference librarians, who can recommend resources and strategies that might save you hours of research time.

Increasingly refined search tools and electronic publications allow you to use similar strategies for Internet searches, in conjunction with electronic library catalogues and databases. It is no longer necessary to sift through hundreds of vaguely related Web sites in search of credible, useful information for academic writing. The "Advanced" options in most Internet search engines offer many ways to locate smaller numbers of more valuable sources, including publications. The "Scholar" option in Google, for example, limits references to academic sources, and further advanced options allow you to restrict and refocus searches by language, field of study, date of publication, and other factors. Clicking the "Citation" feature below a useful source will show you the other publications that have cited that reference, leading you to further, related references on the topic.

And these Internet searches may lead you to the campus library or to its electronic systems. Most college and university libraries subscribe to electronic databases such as LexisNexis and ProQuest, which give students access to a great variety of published material. Reference librarians and library Web sites can show you how to use these systems efficiently.

The syllabus for your course might list excellent references among supplementary readings, allowing you to avoid messy library and Internet searches altogether. When you have identified a general topic, it is also a good idea to ask your professor for a couple of central sources and for help finding a focus. Teachers usually recommend research questions they find interesting, increasing the chances that your papers will meet expectations that were not stated in the assignment.

A Note on Wikipedia

College professors have never been impressed by the use of encyclopedia entries as sources of information in research papers, even when the information and surrounding ideas are sound. They are much more disapproving, as a rule, of papers that cite Wikipedia entries, and many teachers now ban the use of this online encyclopedia as an unreliable, unstable, and entirely too convenient reference. As research specialists, professors distrust the idea that anyone can contribute and revise Wikipedia entries, and because these revisions are ongoing, entries you cite in a paper may have changed by the time your teacher reads your work. Even when the information you find is accurate and useful (as it usually is, due to extensive screening), college teachers tend to view Wikipedia citations as admissions of laziness. If you use this resource at all, therefore, you should use it skeptically and for reference to more reliable (or at least reputable) sources on the topic.

Read Sources and Take Notes

The problem. The linear Standard Method encourages writers to assemble a pile of reference material without reading and then to do all of the reading and note taking before they begin to plan and compose a draft. Completing these tasks in separate stages might seem to be the most efficient, orderly way to get the paper written, but it is not. If you gather all of your references before you read them, you will have no way of evaluating this material, yet your paper will depend on its quality. Separating these procedures will also discourage you from narrowing and focusing your topic during your research, since the pile of references you accumulated will represent your first thoughts, and specific questions you want to pursue will require further searches for different types of information.

In turn, if you try to complete your reading and note taking before you begin to develop a plan for writing and a viewpoint of your own, at the end of the reading stage you will be left with notes on what *other* writers have said. Then you will tend to base your outline on these categories of information, not on your own perspective. Your own voice, viewpoint, and reasons for writing will get sidelined and subordinated to those of other writers, if they develop at all.

Instead, gathering and reading research materials should gradually give you a sense of authority on the subject, a particular viewpoint, and a voice with which you can explain this viewpoint to the reader. *When you begin to write, you should not feel that all you have to say is what other writers have said in the references you cite or that you are writing the paper directly from your notes.* Aimless, passive reading through piles of references can waste enormous amounts of time and leave you with a collection of random notes of uncertain value.

Solutions. A research paper assignment is the ideal occasion for you to practice what I called "predatory reading" in Chapter 3: deliberately searching for and extracting the information you need through a variety of reading strategies. And you should use these strategies throughout your research and writing, not just in a single stage of the process.

Start with one or two of the best sources you can find. Read them first, using this reading both to focus your topic and to identify other sources. You might want to read some sections of a book thoroughly for background information and take extensive notes but to scan or completely ignore sections that are not relevant to your work. In other words, you should always read with a purpose in mind — to find specific information, to acquire background knowledge, to identify research questions, or to understand an author's position—and choose a reading strategy that serves this purpose. If you always read with a specific purpose, you will also know what to write in your notes, and these notes will differ according to your goals: *detailed information, broad perspectives, questions the source raises, summaries of an author's position,* or *relevant quotations.*

The traditional version of the Standard Method placed peculiar emphasis on note cards, as though research, thinking, and writing could be reduced to tidy bookkeeping or a sort of card trick. When you record information in your research, it really doesn't matter where you record your notes as long as you can locate the information and sources again while you are writing. Whether you use note cards, notebooks, or a laptop computer, it is important to keep notes on particular sources separate, with full bibliographical references recorded at the top: (1) *the author's full name;* (2) *the full title of the work;* (3) *the publisher's name and city;* (4) *the year of publication;* (5) *the volume, issue, and page numbers for articles in periodicals;* and (6) *the page numbers, editor's name, and volume title for essays within a book.*

In your notes you should remember to record specific page numbers for quotations, paraphrases, and other material you might cite in the text. You should also be sure to put quotation marks around direct quotes so that you can later distinguish the author's words from your own paraphrases and observations. This careful, bibliographical record keeping will save you from annoying returns to the library when you are documenting sources.

This advice applies equally to electronic sources. When you have taken notes from a Web site, for example, it will seem most efficient at the moment simply to bookmark the page. When you are including citations and assembling a bibliography, however, finding those references can be difficult and time-consuming, especially if you fail to label these bookmarks clearly.

Your notes should include not only what references say but also what *you* are thinking during this research. What questions come to mind? How are your references related? How are your plans for the paper taking shape? I recommend that you keep notes on your own perspectives on cards or pages separate from quotations and other direct references to sources or that you enclose your own thoughts in parentheses, as I did in the following example. In other words, while you are doing research, you should think of yourself as an author, with her own emerging ideas and voice, separate from those of the authors you read. If your thoughts are scattered among references to others, it will be difficult to keep track of them as a cohesive whole, to distinguish them from references, or perhaps even to find them when you begin to write.

> Brumberg, Joan Jacobs. <u>Fasting Girls: The History of Anorexia Nervosa.</u>
> New York: New American Library. 1989.
>
>   Brumberg's view of eating disorders includes historical and cultural
> perspectives. The development of anorexia as "addiction to starvation"
> involves a combination of cultural, biological, and psychological factors
> that determine which individuals are vulnerable in a particular time
> (38). But the terms and meanings change from one period to another.
> (Contrast with Chernin)
>   "Simply put, when and where people become obesophobic and dieting
> becomes pervasive, we can expect to see an escalating number of
> individuals with anorexia nervosa and other eating disorders" (40).
>   Wealth and class are also factors, because food means something
> beyond nutritional needs.
>   "In affluent societies the human appetite is unequivocally misused
> in the service of a multitude of nonnutritional needs. As a result, both
> anorexia nervosa and obesity are characteristic of modern life and will
> continue to remain so" (269).
>   (Is this completely true? Affluence isn't just modern. Check for other
> periods and cultures where food had other meanings—obesity and
> thinness valued?)

    Writers who are studying several sources at once sometimes prefer
to record bibliographical information on separate index cards or on a
master list of references and then code these references on their notes
by number or letter. Then you can simply write "8" or "G" above notes
on that source, along with specific page numbers, and the code will
refer you to your index of sources when you are writing the paper. That
index will also be a handy resource for writing the bibliography.

Construct an Outline

The problem.   Writers often imagine that if they can sort their research
notes into categories and construct an outline, the task of organization is complete. All they need to do is follow the outline. They are
often bewildered, then, when a teacher says the paper is disorganized,
without real direction or focus. In fact, clustering reference material
under the subheadings of an outline won't ensure that the paper will
be cohesive, even if the outline lists a logical series of topics. Because

it represents your initial thoughts about the structure of the paper, an outline can even *prevent* you from seeing new connections and directions while you write if you follow the outline too strictly.

Solutions. As I said in Chapter 4, the use of formal outlines is really a matter of preference—and maybe of personality. Good writing (and bad writing) can occur with or without outlines, and this is true even for long research papers. Whether or not you use a formal outline, you should begin to develop plans for writing *while* you are doing the research, not afterward. *When you have finished most of your reading, therefore, you should have a clear question that you intend to address, a point of departure, a direction, and a destination.*

Some writers like to make a map of this route before they begin to compose. If you begin with the intention of revising your first draft, however, you will give yourself the freedom to explore the topic further as you write and can substantially reorganize the paper in the second version. While you are writing, your perspective might shift, and stronger, more focused viewpoints might emerge toward the end of the paper. For this reason, outlines for research papers, as for other kinds of writing, are often most useful *between* drafts to help you identify a new thesis, move it toward the beginning of the paper, and restructure what follows.

Write the Paper, Incorporating Source Material

The problem. Research papers that are written directly from notes in one draft account for most of the complaints I hear from professors that the papers they receive at the end of the term are unfocused and carelessly written. The "card trick" approach can undermine your work in two related ways:

1. If you write directly from your notes, you will tend to lose your voice and authority as the author of the paper. The paper will become a collection of references to other writers and other authorities, without the cohesion and direction writers establish from a clear point of view.

2. Without a clear voice and viewpoint of your own, you will have trouble distinguishing your language and ideas from those of other writers. As a consequence, figuring out when you should cite references will be difficult.

The resulting paper is little more than a collection of paraphrases and quotations of source material, with or without citation. For reasons explained in Chapter 7, writers in this dilemma tend either to cite almost everything or to cite almost nothing, and in the latter case they often drift into forms of plagiarism. Because they have no voice with which they can easily refer to other writers, they also tend to drop quotations into the middle of their own passages so that the reader cannot identify the author without looking up the citation. Here is an example of a dropped quotation or "mysterious voice" in the first draft of a research paper:

> *Stress is defined as "the pattern of specific and nonspecific responses an organism makes to stimulus events that disturb its equilibrium and tax or exceed its ability to cope" (Zimbardo, 472).*

In this sentence, the passive verb *is defined* suggests that everyone defines stress in this way and that the particular author of this definition is irrelevant. Using the dropped quotation, the writer abdicated her responsibility for choosing to present this particular definition to her readers.

Solutions.   If you've followed my advice thus far, by the time you begin to compose a full draft you should have thought and learned enough about a focused research question to explain what you have discovered to someone else, without referring to your notes. Obviously, you won't recall all of the details, but if you imagine that someone has asked you your research question ("How do beavers decide which trees to cut down?"; "Why did rice production create a market for African slaves?"), you should be able to reply with a coherent explanation or argument. In other words, *you have become an authority on the topic,* and if you need to supplement your explanation with references to other authorities, you know where to find them.

This is the best way to make sure you are approaching the task with authority and a voice of your own. If you feel mute on the subject without your research notes, you are not in a position to write, and your paper will probably turn into a patchwork of references. If you can explain the subject to a listener in your own words, you can also explain it to a reader. While you are writing, then, you will recognize when you need to refer to other authorities or find specific information that supports your explanation. Information from other writing and the voices of other writers can only appear in your paper because you have *chosen* to include them for your own reasons. You have decided to let the reader know, by paraphrase or quotation, what these other writers have said. You are in charge of this paper and are responsible for its quality.

If you are explaining the subject to the reader primarily in your own words, integrating quotations and other references will also seem more natural. As the author of this paper, you will be telling the reader what another writer had to say. In her revision, therefore, the writer who used the preceding "dropped quotation" established her own voice and introduced the definition much more effectively:

> In his book Psychology and Life, *Philip Zimbardo defines stress as "the pattern of specific and nonspecific responses an organism makes to stimulus events that disturb its equilibrium and tax or exceed its ability to cope" (472).*

Even if your teacher does not ask you to submit a rough draft, you should begin to write early enough to revise your paper. The most effective research papers are almost always rewritten because the sharpest focus and the best ideas will usually occur while you are composing a draft, often toward the end. You must be willing to reorganize the paper around a new viewpoint, and toward that end you need to reserve time.

Document References and Add a Bibliography

The problem.   As I've said before, a research paper is simply a long form of an essay or a report based on readings and other references that are used to support an explanation or argument. In terms of methods and responsibilities for documentation, there is not much difference between a five-page paper that refers to three sources and a twenty-page paper that refers to fifteen sources. We can think of the first as a short research paper or of the second as a long essay.

Nonetheless, the number of sources involved and the emphasis teachers often place on documentation may lead you to view this responsibility as an additional, peculiar feature of research papers. And when you think of references and documentation as added features that you have to insert *after* you have written the paper, the idea that a research paper is an alien, complicated type of writing becomes a self-fulfilling prophecy. Figuring out where you got the information you included, what you should cite, where, and how becomes a complex and time-consuming puzzle.

Solutions.   If you followed my advice in Chapter 7, you should have *introduced* and *integrated* references to sources while you were composing a draft, making alterations as necessary in your revisions. Reference, including citation, is then a natural part of writing—for the purpose of distinguishing your voice and ideas from those of others—and is not a separate stage in the process. Reference to others should be a necessary part of writing clearly.

Of course, you should check those references and citations for accuracy as you revise and complete your paper, adding missing information if necessary. And writers usually do assemble a Works Cited list toward the end of the process when they know exactly which references remain in the final version. If you have included thorough bibliographical information in your research notes or kept a separate list of sources with this information, however, composing your Works Cited page should be easy. When you assemble this list of references, just follow the format for the documentation system you are using.

Above all, don't let the technicalities of documentation intimidate you or distract you from the more important challenges of developing a substantial, cohesive, informative research paper. Although you need to use a format for citation consistently and accurately, the great majority of your teachers will be more concerned with the quality of your research and writing than with the details of your documentation. Inconsistent methods of citation can be annoying, especially if we want to find work the writer mentions, but perfect adherence to a format will not redeem a paper that has little to say.

Check for Errors and Typos, and Turn It In

The problem.   Considering the length and importance of these assignments, you might expect that the research papers students turn in would be more polished than their shorter papers, but they frequently contain more errors and typos. Procrastination, I suspect, is the main reason for this carelessness. Students routinely underestimate the time required to finish a long paper and find themselves completing the documentation and bibliography late in the night before the deadline. Under these circumstances it is tempting to assume that careful proof-reading is unnecessary beyond a quick spelling check.

Careless errors, however, will create the more general impression of careless writing and thinking. When teachers encounter lots of spelling errors, typos, poor word choices, and other signs that the writer isn't paying attention to detail, they rarely consider a paper to be first-rate, even if the ideas within it are brilliant. Weak effort at the end of the process, therefore, can undermine your best efforts in other phases of research and writing.

Solutions. The obvious (and only) solution is to allow sufficient time to read the paper carefully—aloud—preferably a day after you have finished the final draft.

Do not trust spell checking and proofreading software to do this work for you! These systems can help you identify errors and other local weak-nesses in a draft, but no experienced writer trusts them entirely. Spell-ing checkers can only identify the words in their internal dictionaries. While proofreading software has improved somewhat in recent years, it still cannot really "understand" written English, identify all errors, or offer reliable advice. As I noted on page 76, electronic proofreaders are especially hazardous for those of you who use English as a second lan-guage, because the errors in usage and syntax that you are most likely to make are the most difficult for a computer program to identify and correct. At best these systems can help you use your own eyes, ears, and sensibilities. At worst they will tell you to change correct sentences into incorrect versions.

Theft, Fraud, and the Loss of Voice

Derived from the Latin word for "kidnapping," *plagiarism* is the theft of someone else's intellectual offspring: their language, ideas, or research. That idea of trying to pass off a stolen child as one's own conveys the seriousness of such offenses in the view of college teachers and admin-istrators. The reason is that words, ideas, and research are the main forms of currency in academic life. Because they represent the "intellec-tual property" with which scholars have built their careers, using that property without permission or credit is a form of larceny. Teachers also assume that the writing and other work students turn in is the prod-uct of their own effort, and because grades (another form of academic currency) are based on that work, "borrowing" language and ideas from someone else without acknowledgment constitutes cheating.

As a consequence, all colleges and universities include warnings against plagiarism among their published rules for academic conduct, along with the procedures and penalties that result from breaking these rules. Because these regulations are usually strict and often unfamiliar to new students, you should read them carefully to make sure you know what practices are prohibited. The most serious forms of plagiarism can lead to failure in a course, notice of misconduct on one's academic record, and even suspension.

Legalistic accounts of plagiarism, however, are also idealistic. In other words, they assume an ideal world in which the boundaries between right and wrong, acceptable and unacceptable practices, one's own language and the language of others, can be clearly defined by regulations. In fact, the term *plagiarism* covers a wide range of deceptions and errors, from serious cases of cheating to minor instances of faulty citation. Violations related to plagiarism also include some types of "unauthorized assistance," and forms of assistance authorized in one course or assignment might be unauthorized in another. Some of the practices that many students consider acceptable "survival strategies" are, for their teachers, punishable offenses. On the Internet, furthermore, authorship and ownership of intellectual property are often unclear. In my effort to clarify these boundaries, therefore, I will also be quite frank about the dilemmas and temptations you are likely to face in your college work.

I'll begin with the most obvious violations of academic integrity codes and end with some deeper, more ambiguous questions about authority, acknowledgment, and originality in academic work—questions that are essential to all writing that is based on research.

Theft and Fraud

The great majority of formal plagiarism charges result from deliberate attempts to deceive teachers, avoid work, and gain an unfair advantage over other students. While these practices share common motives, they take several forms:

- Using published (including electronic) material verbatim, without citation or quotation marks, as all or part of work submitted as one's own. (This category includes not only writing but also quantitative data, graphs, and other published research material.)

- Close, deliberate paraphrase of another author's published or unpublished work without acknowledgment.

- Submitting as your own work papers or portions of papers formerly written by other students or purchased from commercial services.

- Having someone else write a paper for you and turning it in as your own work or writing a paper for someone else.

- Submitting copies of a single paper (written individually or collaboratively) as the individual work of two or more students.

- Turning in a paper you previously wrote for another course, or the same paper for two courses, without permission from the instructors.

When I discover these kinds of deception, I prosecute them without hesitation, as many other teachers do, but I've also learned not to jump to hasty conclusions about the motives and characters of students who resort to plagiarism. Heavy workloads and intense competition sometimes encourage students to use any strategy that gives them an edge, and if substantial numbers adopt this survival-of-the-fittest ethos, more scrupulous, responsible students can get drawn into plagiarism and other forms of cheating to compete.

In a misdirected fashion, some of these violations are also generous. To counter the effects of competition between individuals, students share work and help one another—behavior that would be considered virtuous in other circumstances but is a violation when students are being graded for individual performance. A very bright, capable senior once explained to me, in a completely matter-of-fact way, that freshmen were disadvantaged in a large science course because they didn't yet have access to the sorority and fraternity files of old lab reports and were forced to write their own! Setting ethical questions aside, presenting old lab reports as your own work can be very risky, as many students in that course have discovered. Even when experiments remain basically the same, details of procedures often change, allowing teachers to identify plagiarized versions easily.

These files of old papers, paper-writing and note-taking services, published volumes of student research papers, Cliff Notes, and other easy routes to completing assignments seem to authorize strategies that campus regulations condemn. Internet services make the purchase of "prewritten" term papers entirely too easy and, although selling papers might be legal, turning them in as your own work can violate campus and course policies.

With these and other opportunities available, and with other students using them, what will you do when you are short on time, energy, or ideas, or when you feel that a teacher expects you to write with authority and skills that you don't have? What will you do when you find that a published source says exactly what you would like to say on an assigned topic or when your friend has already written a paper on the subject and offers it to you? You don't have to be morally bankrupt to find plagiarism tempting in such situations.

But each year thousands of otherwise honest, fair-minded students are convicted of plagiarism. One very good reason for avoiding *all* forms of plagiarism is that you might get caught. And if you do, you will find yourself in deep trouble. Frequently and often unpredictably, these cases come to the attention of teachers for reasons that students fail to take into account:

- Teachers are often much more familiar with published sources on a subject than their students realize.

- Many teachers are also attuned to shifts of voice and style, both within a paper and from one paper to the next. They can tell when the author has changed.

- Teachers talk to one another about student work (more than our students know), and we show papers we have received to other teachers, sometimes to get advice.

- If they are suspicious that a paper or portions of it are plagiarized, increasing numbers of teachers use Internet search tools to locate the sources, which they can often find easily with "exact phrase" settings.

This is how charges of plagiarism usually begin, and they can lead to what seems very much like a criminal trial before a committee that serves as judge and jury—examining evidence, hearing testimony, delivering a verdict, and (if the verdict is "guilty") determining penalties. This can be a dreadful ordeal, and no matter how safe and tempting the opportunity to plagiarize might appear to be, it is not worth the risk.

Unauthorized Assistance or Collaboration

Two types of "theft and fraud" I mentioned represent extreme forms of unauthorized assistance or collaboration: turning in someone else's writing as your own and using one paper to represent the work of more than one person. Providing your own work for these purposes represents complicity in these forms of plagiarism.

In other forms, however, the boundaries between acceptable and unacceptable collaboration are not always so clear. Most of us want our students to discuss course material outside class, share ideas and information, and help one another to grasp important concepts. Collaborative learning methods have become increasingly common in higher education, especially in fields of the sciences, engineering, and business. When you graduate, most of you will need to work closely with others toward common goals, including the production of reports and other documents. Most teachers show drafts of our writing to colleagues and rely on one another for substantial help before we send our work to publishers.

For these reasons, teachers often explicitly *authorize* assistance or collaboration on research projects, lab reports, and problem sets. Writing teachers frequently advise students to exchange drafts of their papers, to help one another with revision in pairs or small groups, and to visit writing centers.

But the value of cooperation sometimes conflicts with the value of individual effort. I know a science major who was formally charged with plagiarism for receiving unauthorized help from a friend on the revision of a paper for a humanities course. Collaborative writing is very common in the sciences, where students might also work together on problem sets, labs, other research projects, and reports. But individual authorship is the norm in the humanities, and teachers in fields such as English, history, or philosophy tend to assume that a paper will represent the work of a single writer.

Because collaboration is such a valuable life skill and aid to learning, I do *not* advise you categorically to avoid helping one another with assignments out of fear that you will violate rules. I encourage you instead to *make sure that you know where the boundaries between authorized and unauthorized assistance lie in every course, with awareness that these boundaries will differ*. If a teacher, course syllabus, or assignment does not make these expectations clear, ask for clarification.

Lazy Citation and Paraphrase

Years ago I knew a teacher who became embattled with his small class of six students over an elaborate research paper he assigned in stages similar to the Standard Method: topic selection, a note card system for recording information, outlines, first drafts, and so on. The teacher became very fussy about these procedures, and his students were resistant to his demands. At the end of the semester the students were supposed to turn in their finished papers along with all of their note cards, outlines, and drafts. Then I saw the teacher heading off to the library with all of this material in a cardboard box, intending to look up every reference and to check every quotation, citation, and page number.

When he had completed this onerous task, he charged five of the six students with plagiarism. Because he presented evidence that the students did violate the campus code, his department had to pursue the charges, which were upheld in the hearing.

The most serious offense was a passage copied directly from a source without quotation marks or citation. Even in this case, however, the student claimed that he had plagiarized accidentally by failing to use quotation marks on his note card and therefore assuming, when he wrote the paper, that the writing was his own. There were also individual sentences and phrases borrowed from sources, uncomfortably close paraphrases without acknowledgment, a quotation from one source attributed to another, and inaccurate titles or page numbers. Because most of these violations were minor, the students were sentenced only to rewrite the papers.

Because these cases resulted partly from bad relations in the class, the teacher and students were probably equally to blame for the resulting "plagiarism." In the end, however, the students had to bear the consequences of their careless documentation, and if all college teachers became equally fanatical about the rules for citation and quotation, I suspect that they could find similar kinds of faulty reference in a large proportion of student research papers.

When you are writing under time constraints and find a passage in a source that says essentially what you want to say, when you find a useful quotation in your notes but didn't record the source, or when you forgot to write down the page number for a reference you need, what should you do?

You should (1) either quote the source directly or cite it after your own paraphrase; (2) either find the missing reference or not use the quotation at all; or (3) go back to the reference and find the page number. I realize that these efforts might seem to be a big waste of time and that the chances of a teacher noticing a faulty reference may be slim, but a larger question is involved, regardless of your attitudes toward the teacher and the task: What kind of student, scholar, and writer do you *want* to be?

Accurately crediting and documenting the work of others will be essential in most of the professions you pursue, and if you maintain high standards now, you will learn to keep track of this information carefully in the future. Habits of carelessness and disregard, in turn, are difficult to break.

Loss of Voice

In Chapter 7 and in other sections of this chapter, I've explained how misconceptions about documentation, the failure to introduce and integrate references, and the Standard Method for completing research papers can result in accidental forms of plagiarism. And throughout these chapters, I've emphasized the importance of establishing a voice and perspective of your own. If you believe that a citation at the end of a paragraph authorizes all uses of a source, for example, your readers will not be able to distinguish your voice and ideas from those of referenced authors. This ambiguity often raises suspicions of plagiarism and leads teachers to check original sources.

If you haven't established your own authority over the subject and a reason for writing, it will be difficult for *you* to identify the boundaries between your ideas and language and those of other writers. What you have to say will be what others have already said. Everything you write will come directly from sources and will seem to need citation. In their effort to avoid these strings of citations, students who are writing directly from research notes often drift into plagiarism, closely paraphrasing sources without citing them or "borrowing" exact phrases and sentences without quotation.

The most common forms of plagiarism in student writing therefore result from the loss of voice, which results in turn from misunderstandings, insecurities, or time pressures more often than from deception. For these weaknesses, the term *plagiarism*—which suggests criminal intention and deliberate violation of ethical standards—may seem inappropriate and unfair. Student writers should not be charged with the equivalent of theft and fraud for problems that result from their lack of knowledge, confidence, or experience. In some cases, this distinction is also culturally ambiguous for students who were raised in educational traditions that value imitation, including copying, as legitimate and necessary ways of learning.

When they observe that students have simply pieced together the language and ideas of other writers, however, teachers have no reliable way to determine whether these represent deliberate or accidental misuses of references. Fairly or unfairly, rules of academic integrity refer, like laws, to actions and evidence, even though the causes and motives underlying a violation of these rules may vary.

The best way to avoid these hazards is to make sure you have something you want to say to the reader—something you could generally explain in your own words without relying on your references or notes. This may seem counterintuitive—that to use references effectively, you should be able to write or speak about the subject without using these references at all. When people have something they really want to communicate to others from their own perspectives, however, they always establish their voices for this purpose and distinguish their words and ideas from those of other people they may refer to. They will not tolerate confusion about who thinks and says what. Established methods and rules of reference serve this purpose of clear communication. When writers have nothing to say, however, these methods and rules appear to be pointless formalities.

In academic writing, you can address the reader effectively in your own voice, even when you are summarizing readings, without using the first person or taking a strong position. Here is the beginning of a finished research paper in which the writer has clearly introduced focused research questions, established her own voice, integrated quotations and references appropriately, and set a direction for further discussion. Elizabeth Tricomi wrote this paper on the roles of "working memory" in learning and in mental disorders for an introductory course in cognitive science:

> *What limits our capacity to learn? Why don't we have unlimited access to the supposedly infinite number of memories stored in our long-term memory (LTM)? And what prevents those with serious disorders from learning and remembering normally? Part of the answers to those questions lie in working memory (WM), a model for short-term memory first proposed in 1978 by Alan Baddeley and Graham J. Hitch. Baddeley*

*(1986) describes working memory as a "system for the temporary hold-
ing and manipulation of information during the performance of a range
of cognitive tasks such as comprehension, learning, and reasoning." The
capacity for learning and memory depends on the amount of information
one can manipulate simultaneously in WM. Working memory is used for
everyday cognitive tasks, and is our first approach to understanding new
ideas and concepts. Our long-term memory, which derives meaning and
concepts from information, comes into play based on the information
currently stored in WM (Brainerd, 1983). Working memory can be seen
as the "work space" for storing and processing information, and has a
limited capacity for the amount of information it can process.*

*This paper will explore the evidence for working memory and its im-
portance in common cognitive tasks. It will also study how WM affects
development of learning from childhood to maturity, and its gradual de-
terioration in the elderly.*

GUIDELINES

- A college "research paper" is not a single kind of writing, produced
  by a single method. Instead, the most common features of research
  papers are their length, their importance in a course, and the time-
  management skills required to complete them successfully (pp.
  164–66).

- College teachers typically assign research papers to give you an
  experience of real intellectual engagement and inquiry—scholarship—in their fields.

- For this purpose, the Standard Method students learn in high
  school or from their peers will rarely produce research papers that
  meet the expectations of college teachers.

- The problems inherent in the Standard Method and the solutions
  to these problems are explained on pp. 169–83. These problems
  begin with the failure to identify a focused research question or position that defines your interest in the subject and guides your line
  of inquiry. What *you* have to say, with reference to sources, should
  be continually refined and strengthened throughout the process of
  research and writing.

- Because the best research papers result from this ongoing revision of ideas, methods, and drafts, along with careful editing, you will need to schedule this work in stages and avoid procrastination.

- *Plagiarism* refers to violations of academic integrity codes concerning the misuse or misrepresentation of other people's language and "intellectual property." But forms of plagiarism and their motivations vary radically, from deliberate deception and cheating to loss of authorial voice and careless use of references (pp. 183–91).

- To prevent the loss of voice, avoid writing research papers directly from research notes and sources and make sure you have something you want to say to the reader—something you could explain in your own words without relying on references or notes.

Conclusion
The Whole Point of Writing

An especially vigilant astronomy teacher once showed me a student paper he had highlighted in six colors, each for a different Internet source the student had used, without citation, to assemble a paper without having to write one. My first thought about this complicated patchwork of plagiarized material was that the student who produced it was almost laughably devious and naïve. And the outcome was ironic. He had used Internet search tools to locate sources he could piece together to avoid producing his own response to the assignment. Using the same kinds of search tools, his teacher was able to reconstruct a vivid, detailed map of all of the sources this student was trying to conceal.

In the process, however, this student had reduced writing to a counterfeit operation, and he had reduced teaching to detective work. In the end, this reduction was the real misfortune and loss—more tragic than the violation of rules, his failure to acknowledge sources, or his failing grade. For reasons unknown to me, he had devoted considerable amounts of time, thought, and skill to defeating the whole point of the assignment: the opportunity for him to communicate what *he* had to say about the topic. In his determination to say nothing, he chose to let other writers speak for him. In appropriating their voices, he permitted them to appropriate his voice.

In such cases of deception and in our concerns about dishonesty, we tend to forget about the second half of this equation: that writers have sacrificed their own voices, have chosen not to say anything, and have let others speak for them. This choice contradicts a fundamental purpose of higher education and of writing within higher education: to give individuals *more* to say, with broader perspectives and stronger voices of their own with which they can take more active, constructive roles in professions and public life. Codes of academic integrity emphasize and penalize some ways of defeating this purpose through fraudulent uses of language, ideas, and voices that belong to others.

But there are other, "legal" ways of defeating the central purposes of writing and learning.

In the case of the astronomy paper, for example, we could remove the elements of deception—the risk of plagiarism—without much change in the value of this work. In other words, the student could have quoted and acknowledged the same sources in a patchwork of documented references and missed the point of the assignment just as completely. Consider this second example, which has nothing to do with concealing or misusing sources.

Because his teacher was dissatisfied with his previous essays, a student talked with me about a paper he was just beginning to write—a review of a translation of an ancient religious text. His teacher had been most concerned that the student failed to make his own views clear in his previous papers, so I began by asking him what he thought about the book he was supposed to discuss. Without hesitation, he told me this was an especially impressive form of translation, very different from others he had read. Supporting this view, he explained that both the author's introduction and the detailed annotations of the translated passages always illuminated the original text and turned translation into an ambitious, enlightening work of scholarship. Here was a strong, clear, interesting viewpoint he could use for structuring the paper—exactly what his teacher found missing in his previous work.

When this student showed me the notes he had taken in preparation for writing, however, his own thoughts about the book were completely absent. These notes consisted entirely of quotations from the book that he was supposed to write about. Prepared only to summarize and repeat what he had read, ignoring his own voice and ideas, he was about to miss the point of the assignment once again. After our conversation, however, he based his paper on the views he had expressed to me, using examples and quotations to illustrate his own ideas. And because this was the real purpose of the assignment, his grade rose abruptly from Cs and a D on earlier essays to an A on this one.

Throughout this book, I've argued that the main challenges of adjustment to writing, reading, and learning in college result more often from misconceptions and inflexible strategies than from lack of ability. The preceding example illustrates one of the most fundamental of these misconceptions: **College students tend to underestimate the values their teachers place on active learning, critical and creative thinking, and communication of their own ideas.**

One of the most common complaints about student writing, therefore, is that it simply presents a "rehash" of readings or lectures, with no evidence that the writer has *thought about* this material. As the previous example indicates, students' failure to convey their own thoughts about the subjects of their writing does not always, or even usually, result from their inability to think of anything to say. This student had made interesting observations about the assigned reading, and he was able to use these ideas to develop a paper that his teacher appreciated. Until I intervened, however, he was preparing to ignore those observations (along with his teacher's stated expectations) and to write a "rehash" of the book. Why would he, along with many other students, make this mistake? There are several possible, related explanations:

- He didn't feel that his own ideas or "opinions" were worthy of expression, especially as the central ideas of a paper.
- He didn't want to take the risk of being wrong.
- He believed that a "review" of a book should just summarize its content.
- His conditioned methods of writing and reading, along with his conceptions of an essay, excluded the establishment of his own voice and perspective.

The same explanations usually apply to students who tell me they *don't* have ideas of their own about the subject or that they *can't* think of anything to say beyond what authors and teachers have already said. They may imagine that the problem resides in their lack of knowledge or ability, but the real causes lie in their approaches to reading, writing, and learning. Because passive reading and highlighting emphasize what authors thought and said (as I observed in Chapter 3), these efforts to absorb the content of a text can discourage you from *having* thoughts about the subject or lead you to dismiss such thoughts as irrelevant distractions. Standard methods of completing essays and research papers (discussed in Chapters 4, 7, and 8) can lead you to assemble quotations, paraphrases, and ideas you've taken from sources and recorded in your notes, without establishing your own voice and perspective as the writer. Without a clear voice in your own writing, you can neither express your ideas about the subject nor distinguish your views from those of other writers.

In the first two years of college, furthermore, introductory courses tend to emphasize the acquisition of basic knowledge necessary for further studies. Students who spend much of their time trying to absorb and remember information in preparation for tests of this knowledge may conclude that learning what experts know and say is the main goal of higher education.

For college teachers, however, such priorities confuse ends with means. From their perspective, basic knowledge is an essential but instrumental foundation for further inquiry, discussion, and writing. Individual opinions hold little value in academic work unless they are grounded in current knowledge and debate, in reference to the views of others. For this reason, teachers are not impressed by students who hold forth on whatever they happen to be thinking at the moment and pretend to know everything, without learning from or listening to anyone else.

Instead, when college teachers refer to exceptionally good students in their classes, they describe active learners who think *about* this material, raise and attempt to answer interesting questions, observe gaps and connections in our knowledge, express their own confusion, and use writing and discussion to communicate their intellectual engagement with the subject.

As I explained in Chapter 1, college teachers maintain these expectations and hopes for their students because they are also scholars. In the fields of study they teach, they have spent large portions of their lives not just acquiring knowledge but also *contributing* to knowledge, in collaboration and communication with others. Both as scholars and as teachers, they are most intrigued by remaining puzzles, unanswered questions, gaps in current knowledge, misunderstandings, unobserved connections, and potential discoveries. We shouldn't be surprised that they most admire the students who share these interests, show potential for advanced studies, and, as professors often say, begin to "think like" scholars and other career professionals in their fields. This is also the main reason for which teachers assign writing: to give you the opportunity to communicate your own thoughts about readings and issues in the course. If they were interested only in the amount of information you could remember, they could find out more efficiently through examinations and avoid reading stacks of papers that try to tell them what they already know.

Your teachers also know, in part from their own experiences as students, that establishing your own voice and perspective in academic writing is not only an extremely important transition to advanced studies and careers but also an extremely difficult transition. In her essay "Writing Political Science," Mary Katzenstein, a professor of government at Cornell, recalls the conceptual obstacles to this transition in her own undergraduate studies:

> *Trusting oneself to know what is interesting and to make critical judgments is the paramount challenge for many freshmen and sophomores in political science, indeed, across the disciplines. By freshman year of college, students are—no less in my day than now—skilled replicators of authorized interpretations. Then, at least as I experienced it, this meant scouring the card catalogue in search of just the right secondary source that would unlock the secrets of the essay assignment due Monday, supplemented by the obscure encyclopedia article. . . . Now it is the urgent combing of the Web with its addictive, ever-enticing sense that with just a little more time, one more set of searches, the crucial clue to an often unspecified problem will be unearthed; in both cases the search is driven by the uneasy quest for assurance that someone who "knows" can tell you what is worth saying. (174)*

Like most college professors, Katzenstein also recalls the moment of transition when academic writing became an act of communication and she moved beyond what teachers often call "school writing," motivated primarily by the need to get assignments done in exchange for grades. She said, "I remember, with still palpable pleasure, the first essay I ever wrote as an undergraduate that felt like it was truly my own. It was not, in fact, until my junior year" (175).

In the first year of college, or even in the second, how can you know "what is worth saying" to experts on subjects you have just begun to study? How can you possibly "think" like them or write like them? And why should you attempt to do so, considering the risks of betraying ignorance, if you don't intend to follow a career in that field?

In other words, how can you move beyond "school writing" when you are, in fact, still in school, writing for the real, immediate purposes of completing assignments on time, meeting teachers' expectations, and maintaining decent grades? When I ask students who are working on papers, "Why are you writing?" they almost invariably say, "Because I have a paper due tomorrow" (or the next day or the following week). Of course, that's a valid, obvious explanation that I can't ignore. I know that without assignments to complete, they wouldn't be writing those papers at all.

Like the all-purpose formulas and methods I've described in this book, however, these immediate, compelling reasons for writing aren't sufficient to produce real communication with readers, because they don't include an essential component of written communication: a writer who has something to say. As a consequence, the narrow motivations of completing schoolwork can't really satisfy the expectations of college teachers, the demands of postcollege careers, or the purposes of education itself.

Nor can these reasons for writing fully satisfy student writers themselves, even if they become adept, as many students do, at piecing together borrowed language and ideas in ways that effectively simulate engagement and satisfy requirements. Even when real communication with the reader seems difficult or circumstantially pointless, finding something that you want to say remains a direction in which you should turn, an intellectual skill you should cultivate, and a measure of your real development as a writer, more substantial than any grades you receive. And you should turn in this direction as soon and as often as you can, even in your first semester of college, because it is the only direction in which the real purposes of writing lie. After all, the ultimate goal of a college education is not just to turn you into a terrific college student.

In the maze of undergraduate course requirements, schedules, assignments, deadlines, and grading systems, this fundamental purpose of writing—to communicate with readers—is very difficult for instructors to teach and for students to grasp. And I conclude with this sense of purpose because its discovery, or rediscovery, is an essential, transformative milestone in the transition to college writing and, at once, to written communication beyond college.

Vanessa, a student in one of my writing classes, began to make this discovery in her sophomore year, when writing entirely for the purpose of completing schoolwork had become a tedious chore. Accustomed to leaving herself out of her own papers, she described these narrow motivations in the passive voice ("subsequent papers are written") or as the motives of "students" in general:

> As the teacher comments more and more on papers, it becomes evident what type of writing that teacher is looking for, and revisions and subse-

quent papers are written to meet those expectations. . . . When forced to choose between developing your own personal style or adapting a style to fit the expectations of a teacher, students often choose to please the teacher in order to get a good grade.

But this strategy did not please her teachers entirely. Vanessa told me that although she worked very hard at saying what she *thought* her teachers wanted her to say, she had never received a grade higher than B+ on a paper. To illustrate her view of writing, she made a diagram that looked something like this:

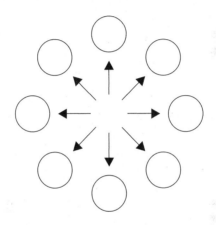

Vanessa explained that the circles represented the various teachers who had assigned papers in her classes. The arrows were her efforts to meet their differing expectations.

I pointed out that she had left the middle of the diagram empty—left herself out of her own description of writing. "But you are actually there," I argued, "at the center of your work, making these efforts, developing these different strategies." When I began to write Vanessa's name in the center of the diagram, however, she stopped me. "No, I don't feel like the writing has anything to do with me," she said. "It just makes me feel exhausted, depleted."

As Vanessa described this view of writing, she also began, in following weeks, to change it: to think of her writing not just as an outcome of teachers' expectations but as something she wanted to say to readers. As this change occurred, she began not only to *think* of writing differently but also to write differently, with greater satisfaction, voice, and presence in her work:

> *I feel as if I'm looking outside through a slightly opened window on a spring day. I can just barely feel a warm breeze, but when I look out the window I see that if I could open it all the way I would not only feel the warm breeze, but I'd also smell the flowers and hear the birds singing. I feel like I'm only experiencing and utilizing a small part of something that can be very powerful, useful, and expressive.*

Works Cited

ACS Style Guide: A Manual for Authors and Editors. 2nd ed. Edited by Janet S. Dodd. New York: American Chemical Society, 1997.

Agee, James, and Walker Evans. *Let Us Now Praise Famous Men.* Boston: Houghton Mifflin, 1988.

"Attitudes and Characteristics of Freshmen at 4-Year Colleges, Fall 2004." *Chronicle of Higher Education Almanac Issue* 52, no. 1 (2005): 18.

Azar, Betty Schrampfer. *Understanding and Using English Grammar.* Englewood Cliffs, NJ: Prentice-Hall, 2001.

Baker, Sheridan. *The Practical Stylist.* 8th ed. New York: Longman, 1998.

Benson, Morton, et al. *The BBI Combinatory Dictionary of English.* Philadelphia: John Benjamins Publishing Company, 1986.

Biber, Douglas, et al. *Longman Grammar of Spoken and Written English.* Essex: Pearson Education Limited, 1999.

———. *Longman Student Grammar of Spoken and Written English.* Essex: Pearson Education Limited, 2002.

Bartholomae, David, and Anthony Petrosky. *Ways of Reading: An Anthology for Writers.* 6th ed. Boston: Bedford/St. Martin's, 2008.

Bennion, Louisa. "'The Snow Is General All Over Ireland': Visions of the Self in Stories by Joyce." *Discoveries* no. 2 (1997): 9–18.

Bergson, Henri. *Creative Evolution.* New York: Henry Holt, 1911.

Bourdieu, Pierre. *Outline of a Theory of Practice.* Cambridge: Cambridge University Press, 1977.

Boyer, Ernest L. *College: The Undergraduate Experience in America.* New York: Harper and Row, 1988.

The Chicago Manual of Style. 15th ed. Chicago: University of Chicago Press, 2003.

Chomsky, Noam. *Language and Mind.* New York: Harcourt, Brace, and World, 1968.

Cohen, Joel. *How Many People Can the Earth Support?* New York: W. W. Norton, 1995.

Davies, Merrill J. "Whistling in the Dark." In *What Is College-Level Writing?* Edited by Patrick Sullivan and Howard Tinberg. Urbana, IL: NCTE, 2006.

Dillard, Annie. *The Writing Life.* New York: Harper Perennial, 1990.

Geertz, Clifford. "The Social Scientist as Author." *Journal of Advanced Composition* 11, no. 2 (1991): 245–68.

Gibaldi, Joseph. *MLA Handbook for Writers of Research Papers.* 6th ed. New York: Modern Language Association, 2003.

Greene, Brian. *The Fabric of the Cosmos: Space, Time, and the Texture of Reality.* New York: Vintage Books, 2005.

Hacker, Diana. *Rules for Writers.* 6th ed. Student Site. http://bcs.bedford stmartins.com/rules6e/Player/pages/Main.aspx.

———. *A Writer's Reference.* 6th ed. Boston: Bedford/St. Martin's, 2007.

Katzenstein, Mary. "Writing Political Science." In *Local Knowledges, Local Practices: Writing in the Disciplines at Cornell.* Edited by Jonathan Monroe. Pittsburgh: University of Pittsburgh Press, 2003.

Lunsford, Andrea, et al. *Everything's an Argument.* 3rd ed. Boston: Bedford/St. Martin's, 2004.

Normile, Dennis. "Asian Fusion." *Science* 312 (May 2006): 993.

Ong, Walter. *Orality and Literacy: The Technologizing of the Word.* London: Methuen, 1982.

Owen, David. "Green Manhattan." *The New Yorker* (October 18, 2004): 111–23.

Parsons, Talcott. *The Structure of Social Action.* New York: The Free Press, 1937.

Perl, Sondra. "Understanding Composing." *College Composition and Communication* 31 (1980): 363–69.

Pinker, Steven. *The Language Instinct.* New York: Harper Perennial, 1995.

Poushkareva, Anastasia. "Genealogy of the Third Reich: The Connection between Nietzschean and Nazi Ideas." *Discoveries* no. 6 (2005): 67–74.

Publication Manual of the American Psychological Association. 5th ed. Washington, DC: American Psychological Association, 2001.

Raimes, Ann. *Keys for Writers.* 4th ed. Boston: Houghton Mifflin, 2004.

———. *Grammar Troublespots: A Guide for Student Writers.* Cambridge: Cambridge University Press, 2004.

Rose, Mike. *Lives on the Boundary.* New York: The Free Press, 1989.

Shocklee, Paul D. "What Is Time?" *Discoveries* no. 1 (1995): 39–43.

Sklar, Robert. *F. Scott Fitzgerald: The Last Laocoön.* New York: Oxford University Press, 1967.

Sommers, Nancy. "Revision Strategies of Student Writers and Experienced Adult Writers." *College Composition and Communication* 31 (1980): 378–88.

———. "Between the Drafts." *College Composition and Communication* 43, no. 1 (1992): 23–31.

Stafford, William. *Writing the Australian Crawl: Views on the Writer's Vocation.* Ann Arbor: University of Michigan Press, 1978.

Stockton, Sharon. "Students and Professionals Writing Biology: Disciplinary Work and Apprentice Storytellers." *Language and Learning across the Disciplines* 1, no. 2 (1994): 80–104.

Thompson, A. J., and A. V. Martinet. *A Practical English Grammar.* Oxford: Oxford University Press, 1986.

Whyte, William F. *Street Corner Society.* Chicago: University of Chicago Press, 1943.

Wilson, Edward O. *The Diversity of Life.* New York: W. W. Norton, 1992.

Yezierska, Anzia. *Bread Givers.* New York: Braziller, 1975.

Index